150 Hearty Homestyle
RECIPES

Gooseberry Patch

An imprint of Globe Pequot
246 Goose Lane
Guilford, CT 06437

www.gooseberrypatch.com
1•800•854•6673

Copyright 2016, Gooseberry Patch 978-1-62093-212-4

Do you have a tried & true recipe...

tip, craft or memory that you'd like to see featured in
a **Gooseberry Patch** cookbook? Visit our website at
www.gooseberrypatch.com and follow the
easy steps to submit your favorite family recipe.
Or send them to us at:

Gooseberry Patch
PO Box 812
Columbus, OH 43216-0812

Don't forget to include the number of servings your recipe makes,
plus your name, address, phone number and email address. If we
select your recipe, your name will appear right along with it...
and you'll receive a **FREE** copy of the book!

Contents

Dedication

To everyone who loves sitting down to a cozy
home-cooked meal with family & friends.

Breakfast & Brunch

Nutty Maple Waffles

Crunchy pecans paired with maple...a great way to begin the day! Top with plenty of butter and rich maple syrup.

1-1/2 c. all-purpose flour
2 T. sugar
1 t. baking powder
1/4 t. salt
2 eggs, separated

12-oz. can evaporated milk
3 T. oil
1/2 t. maple extract
1/2 c. pecans, finely chopped

Combine flour, sugar, baking powder and salt in a medium bowl; mix well and set aside. Combine egg yolks, evaporated milk, oil and extract in a large bowl; stir well. Gradually add flour mixture, beating well after each addition; set aside. In a small bowl, beat egg whites with an electric mixer on high speed until stiff peaks form; fold into batter. For each waffle, pour 1/2 cup batter onto a preheated, greased waffle iron; sprinkle with one tablespoon nuts. Bake according to manufacturer's instructions. Makes 8 servings.

There are so many farmers' markets, antique sales and county fairs year 'round...be sure to visit at least one! A hearty breakfast together with family & friends will start the day off right.

Nutty Maple Waffles

Buttermilk Oven Pancakes

Buttermilk Oven Pancakes

Great for busy mornings...no one has to stand by the stove, flipping pancakes! For a different taste, sprinkle the batter with fresh fruit.

1-1/2 c. all-purpose flour
2 T. sugar
1 t. baking soda
1 t. baking powder
1/4 t. salt

1 egg, beaten
1-1/2 c. buttermilk
3 T. oil
cinnamon-sugar to taste
Garnish: butter, maple syrup

In a bowl, stir together flour, sugar, baking soda, baking powder and salt. In a separate bowl, combine egg, buttermilk and oil; add to dry ingredients. Stir just until mixed, but slightly lumpy. Spread batter evenly in a greased and floured 15"x10" jelly-roll pan. Sprinkle with cinnamon-sugar to taste. Bake at 350 degrees for 16 to 18 minutes, until top springs back when lightly touched and edges are lightly golden. Cut into squares and serve with butter and maple syrup. Makes 4 to 6 servings.

Cook up a yummy topping for pancakes and waffles.
Melt 2 tablespoons butter in a skillet over low heat. Stir in
1/4 cup brown sugar and 2 cups thinly sliced apples.
Cook and stir until tender...delicious!

Sugarplum Bacon

Crunchy, sweet and salty...this bacon is out-of-this-world good!
Cook some up for your brunch guests. They're sure to love it.

1 c. brown sugar, packed
2 t. cinnamon

1 lb. bacon

Combine brown sugar and cinnamon in a bowl; set aside. Cut each bacon slice in half crosswise; dredge in brown sugar mixture. Twist bacon slices and place in 2 ungreased 13"x9" baking pans. Bake at 350 degrees for 15 to 20 minutes, until bacon is crisp and brown sugar is bubbly. Place bacon on aluminum foil to cool. Serve at room temperature. Serves 6 to 8.

Skillet Apples & Sausages

Apples and brown sugar give the sausages such a
delicious sweetness...a great side dish for a brunch.

1 lb. pork breakfast sausage links
6 Golden Delicious apples, cored
   and cut into 8 wedges
3 T. brown sugar, packed

1 T. lemon juice
1/4 t. salt
1/8 t. pepper

In a large skillet over medium heat, cook sausages for about 10 minutes, until no longer pink inside. Drain; cut sausages in half and return to skillet. Add apple wedges; sprinkle with remaining ingredients. Cover and cook over medium-low heat for 10 to 15 minutes, until apples are just tender, gently stirring once or twice. Serves 6.

Sugarplum Bacon

Make-Ahead Breakfast Eggs

Make-Ahead Breakfast Eggs

Savory scrambled eggs for a crowd...perfect for Saturday morning before you go leaf-peeping, antiquing or cheering on your favorite team!

1 doz. eggs, beaten
1/2 c. milk
1/2 t. salt
1/4 t. pepper
1 T. butter

1 c. sour cream
12 slices bacon, crisply cooked
   and crumbled
1 c. shredded sharp Cheddar
   cheese

Beat together eggs, milk, salt and pepper; set aside. In a large skillet, melt butter over medium-low heat. Add egg mixture to skillet. Cook, stirring occasionally, until eggs are set but still moist; remove from heat and cool. Stir in sour cream. Spread mixture in a greased shallow 2-quart casserole dish; top with bacon and cheese. Cover and refrigerate overnight. To serve, uncover and bake at 300 degrees for 15 to 20 minutes, until heated through and cheese is melted. Serves 6 to 8.

13

Crispy potato pancakes are a great way to use up leftover mashed potatoes. Stir an egg yolk and some minced onion into 2 cups mashed potatoes. Form into patties and fry in a little butter until golden. Delicious with all your favorite egg dishes.

Southern Veggie Brunch Bake

Equally delicious at breakfast time or for dinner!

1 lb. ground pork sausage,
   browned and drained
1/2 c. green onions, chopped
1 green pepper, diced
1 red pepper, diced
1 jalapeño pepper, seeded
   and diced
2 tomatoes, chopped

2 c. shredded mozzarella cheese
1 doz. eggs, beaten
1 c. milk
1 c. biscuit baking mix
1/2 t. dried oregano
1/2 t. salt
1/4 t. pepper

In a greased 3-quart casserole dish, layer sausage, onions, peppers, tomatoes and cheese. In a large bowl, whisk together remaining ingredients; pour over cheese. Bake, uncovered, at 350 degrees for 55 to 60 minutes, until set and top is golden. Let stand for 10 minutes before serving. Serves 6 to 8.

Invite the new ne.   ors or the new family at church over for brunch. Send tr.   home with a basket of fresh-baked goodies wrapped ir   towel...such a friendly gesture!

Southern Veggie Brunch Bake

Company Breakfast Casserole

Company Breakfast Casserole

This hearty breakfast bake is perfect to serve to overnight guests anytime.

1/2 lb. bacon
1/2 c. onion, chopped
1 doz. eggs, beaten
1 c. milk
3-1/2 c. frozen shredded
   hashbrowns, thawed

1-1/2 c. shredded sharp Cheddar
   cheese
1 t. salt
1/2 t. pepper

In a skillet over medium heat, cook bacon until crisp. Crumble bacon and set aside, reserving 2 tablespoons drippings. Sauté onion in reserved drippings until tender; set aside. In a bowl, beat together eggs and milk; stir in onion, bacon and remaining ingredients. Spoon into a greased 13"x9" baking pan. Bake, uncovered, at 350 degrees for 40 to 45 minutes, until a knife inserted near the middle comes out clean. Serves 6.

Banana Bread Muffins

*These tasty muffins are just right for brunch or
for tucking into lunchboxes.*

1 c. oil
1 c. sugar
2 eggs, beaten
3 ripe bananas, mashed
1-1/2 c. all-purpose flour

1/2 c. whole-wheat flour
1/2 t. salt
2 to 3 T. lemon juice
2 t. baking soda
1 c. semi-sweet chocolate chips

Blend together oil and sugar in a large bowl; add eggs and bananas and set aside. Mix together flours and salt; stir into oil mixture. Add lemon juice and baking soda; fold in chocolate chips. Spoon batter into greased muffin cups, filling 2/3 full. Bake at 350 degrees for 25 minutes. Makes about 2 dozen.

Ripe Tomato Tart

*Fresh roma tomatoes are available year 'round so you can
enjoy this summery-tasting pie anytime.*

9-inch pie crust
1-1/2 c. shredded mozzarella
   cheese, divided
4 roma tomatoes, cut into wedges
3/4 c. fresh basil, chopped

4 cloves garlic, minced
1/2 c. mayonnaise
1/2 c. grated Parmesan cheese
1/8 t. white pepper

Line a 9" tart pan with pie crust; press crust into fluted sides of pan and
trim edges. Bake at 450 degrees for 5 to 7 minutes; remove from oven.
Sprinkle with 1/2 cup mozzarella cheese; let cool on a wire rack. Combine
remaining mozzarella cheese and other ingredients; mix well and spoon
into crust. Reduce heat to 375 degrees; bake for about 20 minutes, until
bubbly on top. Let stand for 10 minutes before serving. Makes 6 servings.

For a brunch buffet, serve an assortment of artisan cheeses. Line a
white-washed basket with red and white homespun, tie a red bow on
the handle and fill it with a variety of cheeses and crackers. Perfect for
guests to nibble on... they may even discover a new favorite or two!

Ripe Tomato Tart

Sausage-Cranberry Quiche

Sausage-Cranberry Quiche

*The tartness of cranberries combined with spicy sausage
makes a terrific match!*

1/2 lb. sage-flavored ground
   pork sausage
1/4 c. onion, chopped
3/4 c. sweetened dried cranberries
9-inch pie crust

1-1/2 c. shredded Monterey
   Jack cheese
3 eggs, beaten
1-1/2 c. half-and-half

In a large skillet over medium-high heat, brown sausage with onion; drain.
Remove from heat and stir in cranberries. Line a 9" pie plate with pie crust.
Sprinkle cheese into pie crust; evenly spoon in sausage mixture. In a bowl,
combine eggs and half-and-half; whisk until mixed but not frothy. Pour egg
mixture over sausage mixture. Bake at 375 degrees for 40 to 45 minutes,
until a knife tip inserted in the center comes out clean. Let stand for
10 minutes before serving. Makes 6 servings.

Wake-Up Fruit Salad

Add a sprinkle of granola for a crunchy topping.

26-oz. jar mixed fruit, drained
2 ripe bananas, sliced
1 c. blueberries

1/2 c. celery, sliced
1/4 to 1/2 c. poppy seed salad
   dressing

Combine mixed fruit, bananas, blueberries and celery in a bowl. Toss with
dressing. Makes 6 to 8 servings.

Easiest Cinnamon-Raisin Rolls

*Brew a pot of coffee and share these wonderful rolls with
your neighborhood pals.*

2 c. biscuit baking mix
1/2 c. raisins
1/2 c. sour cream
4 T. milk, divided
2 T. butter, softened

1/2 c. brown sugar, packed
1/4 c. walnuts, finely chopped
1/2 t. cinnamon
1 c. powdered sugar

In a bowl, combine biscuit mix, raisins, sour cream and 3 tablespoons milk;
stir just until combined. Gently smooth dough into a ball on a floured tea
towel; knead 10 times. Roll dough into a 12-inch by 10-inch rectangle.
Spread dough with softened butter. Mix brown sugar, walnuts and
cinnamon; sprinkle over dough. Starting on one long edge, roll up dough
tightly; pinch edges to seal. Cut roll into 12 slices. Place slices, cut-side
down, in greased muffin cups. Bake at 400 degrees for 15 minutes, or until
golden. Stir together powdered sugar and remaining milk; drizzle over
warm rolls. Makes one dozen.

A sweet keepsake for a family brunch. Copy one of
Grandma's tried & true recipes onto a festive card,
then punch a hole in the corner and tie the card to
a rolled napkin with a length of ribbon.

Easiest Cinnamon-Raisin Rolls

Raised Doughnuts

Raised Doughnuts

*Nothing compares to an old-fashioned homemade doughnut!
Enjoy with coffee at breakfast...serve with hot spiced
cider at party time.*

2 c. boiling water
1/2 c. sugar
1 T. salt
2 T. shortening
2 envs. active dry yeast

2 eggs, beaten
7 c. all-purpose flour
oil for frying
Garnish: additional sugar
  for coating

Stir water, sugar, salt and shortening together in a large bowl; sprinkle yeast on top. Set aside; cool to room temperature. Stir in eggs; gradually stir in flour. Cover and let rise until double in bulk. On a floured surface, roll out dough 1/2-inch thick; cut with a doughnut cutter. Cover doughnuts and let rise until double in bulk, about 1-1/2 hours. In a deep saucepan, heat several inches of oil to 360 degrees. Fry doughnuts, a few at a time, until golden; drain on paper towels. Spoon sugar into a paper bag; add warm doughnuts and shake to coat. Makes about 4 dozen.

Vanilla Coffee

A rich, mellow wake-up beverage that you're sure to enjoy.

1-1/2 c. milk
1 T. sugar
1/2 t. cinnamon
3 c. hot, strong brewed coffee

1-1/2 t. vanilla extract
Garnish: whipped topping,
  additional cinnamon

Combine milk, sugar and cinnamon in a saucepan and stir well. Cook over medium heat for 2 minutes, or until sugar dissolves. Do not boil. Remove from heat; stir in coffee and vanilla. Pour into mugs; garnish with whipped topping and sprinkle with cinnamon. Serves 4.

Cranberry Tea

A special treat for tea lovers. So yummy with cranberry scones!

6 c. water, divided
2 family-size or 8 regular tea bags
1 t. whole cloves
2 2-1/2 inch cinnamon sticks

2 c. sugar
2 c. cranberry juice cocktail
1 c. orange juice
1/4 c. lemon juice

In a large pot, bring 4 cups water to a boil over medium-high heat. Add tea bags, cloves and cinnamon sticks; cover and steep for 5 minutes. Strain, discarding tea bags and spices. Add remaining water and other ingredients; stir until warmed through and sugar is dissolved. Serve warm or over ice. Makes 4 quarts.

Go out to greet the sunrise! Wrap warm breakfast breads in a vintage tea towel before tucking into a basket... add a thermos of hot coffee or spiced tea.

Cranberry Tea

Mushroom & Sausage Mini Quiches

These mini quiches are so tasty and simple...
perfect for breakfast or a brunch buffet.

8-oz. pkg. turkey breakfast
   sausage links, sliced
1 t. olive oil
8-oz. can sliced mushrooms,
   drained
1/4 c. green onions, sliced

1/4 c. shredded Swiss cheese
1 t. pepper
5 eggs
3 egg whites
1 c. milk

Brown sausage in a skillet over medium-high heat; drain and transfer to a bowl. To the same skillet, add oil and mushrooms. Cook, stirring often, until golden, about 5 to 7 minutes. Add mushrooms to sausage. Stir in green onions, cheese and pepper. In a separate bowl, whisk together eggs, egg whites and milk. Divide egg mixture evenly among 12 lightly greased muffin cups. Sprinkle a heaping tablespoon of sausage mixture into each cup. Bake at 325 degrees for 25 minutes, or until tops are golden. Remove quiches from cups; cool on a wire rack. Makes one dozen.

Mushroom & Sausage Mini Quiches

Frosty Orange Juice

Thick, frosty and very refreshing...a real picker-upper!

6-oz. can frozen orange juice
   concentrate, partially thawed
1 c. milk
1 c. water

1 t. vanilla extract
1/3 c. sugar
12 ice cubes

Process all ingredients together in a blender until frothy. Serve in tall glasses. Makes 4 servings.

A fresh breakfast side dish...fruit kabobs! Just slide pineapple chunks, apple slices, orange wedges and strawberries onto a wooden skewer. They can even be slipped into breakfast smoothies or frosty juices.

Frosty Orange Juice

☕ A jar of honey is a sweet addition to the breakfast table to enjoy on hot biscuits, toast or pancakes...even drizzled in a steamy cup of hot tea. Pick up flavors like orange blossom and wildflower at a farmers' market. Be sure to add a wooden honey dipper too!

☕ Planning a midday brunch? Alongside breakfast foods like baked eggs, coffee cake and cereal, offer a light, savory casserole or a zingy salad for those who have already enjoyed breakfast.

☕ Keep a cozy sweater on a hook near the back door and enjoy an early-morning walk after breakfast.

☕ The time is always right to share some tasty treats with teachers, librarians and school bus drivers...let them know how much you appreciate them.

Appetizers & Salads

Greek Spread

A must for parties...guests are sure to request it!

1 c. plus 1 T. chopped almonds, divided
2 8-oz. pkgs. cream cheese, softened
8-oz. pkg. crumbled feta cheese
7-oz. jar roasted red peppers, drained and chopped
10-oz. pkg. frozen spinach, thawed and drained
1 clove garlic, chopped
snack crackers or toasted pita wedges

Line a 2-quart bowl with plastic wrap; sprinkle in one tablespoon almonds. In a separate bowl, mix together 1/2 cup almonds, cheeses, peppers, spinach and garlic; blend well. Press into bowl over almonds. Cover and chill overnight. Invert onto a serving dish. Remove plastic wrap; press remaining almonds onto the outside. Serve with crackers or pita wedges. Makes about 7 cups.

34

Appetizer spreads are perfect for enjoying during card games or watching sports on TV at home with friends! Set out a variety of creamy dips, crunchy snacks and sweet munchies along with fizzy beverages.

Greek Spread

Tailgating Corn Dip

Tailgating Corn Dip

*This delicious cool dip is a snap to put together! The flavor
is even better if it's made one to two days ahead of time.*

3 11-oz. cans sweet corn & diced
    peppers, drained
7-oz. can chopped green chiles
6-oz. can chopped jalapeño
    peppers, drained and liquid
    added to taste
1/2 c. green onions, chopped

1 c. mayonnaise
1 c. sour cream
1 t. pepper
1/2 t. garlic powder
16-oz. pkg. shredded sharp
    Cheddar cheese
scoop-type corn chips

In a large bowl, mix together all ingredients except corn chips. Cover and
refrigerate until serving time. Serve with corn chips. Makes about 6 cups.

Favorite Easy Salsa

Serve with tortilla chips or add to your favorite Mexican dish.

14-1/2 oz. can petite diced
    tomatoes, drained
4-oz. can diced green chiles
1/2 c. onion, finely chopped

1 T. red wine vinegar
1 t. sugar
1/8 t. salt

Combine all ingredients in a bowl; stir. Cover and chill. Let stand 30 minutes
at room temperature before serving. Makes 2 cups.

Buffalo Wing Dip

A hearty, zesty dip that's just right for a tailgating party.
Be prepared to bring home an empty pan!

2 8-oz. pkgs. cream cheese,
   softened
15-oz. jar chunky blue cheese
   salad dressing
12-oz. bottle chicken wing sauce

2 boneless, skinless chicken
   breasts, cooked and shredded
8-oz. pkg. shredded Cheddar Jack
   cheese
tortilla chips or assorted crackers

In a bowl, blend together cream cheese and salad dressing until smooth. Spread in the bottom of an ungreased 8"x8" baking pan. Combine sauce and chicken; spoon over cream cheese mixture. Sprinkle with shredded cheese. Bake, uncovered, at 350 degrees for 20 minutes, or until cheese is melted and dip is heated through. Serve with tortilla chips or crackers. Serves 10.

Warm Artichoke Dip

This dip is so good, you'll want to eat it right from the oven...
but do let it cool just a bit first!

2 6-oz. cans marinated artichokes,
   drained and coarsely chopped
1/2 c. mayonnaise
1-1/2 c. shredded Parmesan
   cheese
1-1/2 c. shredded mozzarella
   cheese

8-oz. pkg. cream cheese, softened
1/2 c. onion, chopped
2 cloves garlic, pressed
salt and pepper to taste
Optional: 1-1/2 t. prepared
   horseradish
shredded wheat crackers

Combine all ingredients except crackers; spread in a lightly greased 13"x9" baking pan. Bake, uncovered, at 350 degrees for 45 minutes, or until bubbly and golden on top. Serve warm with crackers for dipping. Serves 8 to 12.

Buffalo Wing Dip

Maple Chicken Wings

Maple Chicken Wings

The tasty maple and Dijon marinade makes these wings extra special.

2 to 3 lbs. chicken wings,
   cut into sections
1 c. pure maple syrup
2/3 c. chili sauce

1/2 c. onion, finely chopped
2 T. Dijon mustard
2 t. Worcestershire sauce
1/4 to 1/2 t. red pepper flakes

Place wings in a large plastic zipping bag; set aside. For marinade, combine remaining ingredients in a bowl. Reserve one cup of marinade for basting; refrigerate until ready to use. Pour remaining marinade over wings, turning to coat. Seal bag; refrigerate for 4 hours, turning occasionally. Drain wings, discarding marinade. Place wings in a lightly greased 13"x9" baking pan. Bake, uncovered, at 375 degrees for 30 to 40 minutes, basting with reserved marinade, until golden and juices run clear when pierced. Makes 2 to 3 dozen.

Wondering what's the best way to cut up slippery chicken wings? A pair of sturdy kitchen scissors can do the job in a jiffy. Afterwards, wash the scissors well in soapy water and set on a towel to dry.

Mini Sausage Tarts

These savory tarts look so fancy on an appetizer tray...your friends will never know how easy they are to make!

1 lb. ground pork sausage,
  browned and drained
8-oz. pkg. shredded Mexican-blend
  cheese
3/4 c. ranch salad dressing

2 T. black olives, chopped
4 pkgs. 15-count frozen mini
  phyllo cups
Optional: diced red peppers,
  diced black olives

In a large bowl, combine sausage, cheese, salad dressing and olives; blend well. Divide among phyllo cups; arrange on ungreased baking sheets. If desired, sprinkle tarts with diced peppers and olives. Bake at 350 degrees for 10 to 12 minutes, until golden and cheese is melted. Serve warm. Makes 5 dozen.

Scoop out the centers of cherry tomatoes, then fill with a dollop of a flavorful, creamy dip. Lighter than crackers and chips...sure to be appreciated by guests!

Mini Sausage Tarts

3-Cheese Artichoke Bites

3-Cheese Artichoke Bites

Mini appetizers filled with Cheddar, Parmesan and mozzarella cheese...scrumptious!

1 onion, chopped
1 clove garlic, minced
1 T. oil
6 eggs, beaten
2 6-1/2 oz. jars marinated
  artichokes, drained and chopped
1 c. shredded Cheddar cheese
1 c. shredded mozzarella cheese

1 c. grated Parmesan cheese
1/4 c. fresh parsley, chopped
1/2 t. Italian seasoning
1/4 t. pepper
1/8 t. Worcestershire sauce
1/8 t. hot pepper sauce
1/4 c. Italian-seasoned dry
  bread crumbs

In a skillet over medium heat, sauté onion and garlic in oil until tender; drain and set aside. Combine eggs, artichokes, cheeses, parsley, seasonings and sauces in a large bowl; mix well. Stir in onion mixture and bread crumbs. Fill greased mini muffin cups 2/3 full. Bake at 325 degrees for 15 to 20 minutes, until firm and golden. Serve warm. Makes 3-1/2 to 4 dozen.

45

Garlic Pretzels

It's hard to stop eating these savory nuggets!

4 12-oz. pkgs. Bavarian-style
  pretzels, coarsely broken
12-oz. bottle butter-flavored
  popping oil

2 1-1/2 oz. pkgs. onion
  soup mix
2 t. garlic powder

Place pretzels in a large roasting pan; set aside. In a bowl, combine remaining ingredients; pour over pretzels and toss to coat. Bake, uncovered, at 350 degrees for 20 minutes, stirring every 5 minutes. Spread pretzels on paper towels to cool. Store in an airtight container. Makes 6 cups.

Cheese Straws

These crunchy treats are an old Southern tradition...
sure to be welcome on any party table!

16-oz. pkg. shredded sharp
  Cheddar cheese, room
  temperature
1-1/4 c. margarine, softened

3 c. all-purpose flour
1 t. cayenne pepper
1 t. salt

Combine all ingredients in a large bowl. Mix well, using your hands.
Spoon dough into a cookie press with a star tip. Press dough in strips onto
ungreased baking sheets; cut strips 3 inches long. Bake at 350 degrees for
12 to 15 minutes, until orange on bottom and around edges. Cool on wire
racks; store in an airtight container. Makes 3 to 4 dozen.

Planning an appetizers-only event? You'll want to serve at least 5
different dishes...allow 2 to 3 servings of each per person.

Cheese Straws

Tomato-Garbanzo Salad

Tomato-Garbanzo Salad

*Next time you're looking for something new to take
to a get-together, try this tasty salad.*

1 c. elbow macaroni, uncooked
15-oz. can garbanzo beans,
   drained and rinsed
2 c. tomatoes, diced
1 c. celery, diced
1/2 c. red onion, diced

1/3 c. olive oil
1/4 c. lemon juice
2 T. fresh parsley, chopped
2 t. ground cumin
2 t. salt
1/2 t. pepper

Cook macaroni according to package directions; drain and rinse in cold
water. Transfer macaroni to a large bowl. Add remaining ingredients;
stir to mix well. Cover and chill at least one hour before serving. Makes
6 servings.

Old-fashioned canning jars are perfect for
toting individual salad servings to picnics
or family get-togethers.

Creamy Cucumber Crunch

*A dreamy dressing and the satisfying crunch of fresh veggies...
always a hit at tailgating cookouts.*

8 cucumbers	1/2 c. fresh dill, chopped and
1 t. salt	loosely packed
6 radishes, thinly sliced	2 T. lime juice
8-oz. container plain yogurt	1/4 t. pepper
1/2 c. sour cream	1 clove garlic, pressed

Remove several strips of peel from each cucumber; cut in half lengthwise.
Scoop out seeds and thinly slice each half crosswise. Toss cucumbers with
salt in a large bowl; set aside for 30 minutes. Combine remaining
ingredients in a separate large bowl; mix well and set aside. Drain
cucumbers, pressing to remove as much liquid as possible. Pat dry with
paper towels. Add cucumbers to radish mixture and toss until evenly
coated. Cover and chill for at least one hour to overnight. Serves 10.

Use mini cookie cutters or a crinkle cutter to jazz up zucchini,
carrots, radishes and other sliced veggies for appetizer trays.
Keep extra veggie dippers crisp in the fridge by wrapping them
in damp paper towels and storing in a plastic zipping bag.

Creamy Cucumber Crunch

Peppy 4-Bean Salad

Peppy 4-Bean Salad

This colorful salad is sure to be popular at your next potluck!

14-1/2 oz. can green beans,
   drained
14-1/2 oz. can yellow beans,
   drained
15-1/2 oz. can kidney beans,
   drained
16-oz. can lima beans, drained
14-1/2 oz. can sliced carrots,
   drained

1 green pepper, diced
1 red onion, diced
1 c. celery, diced
1/2 c. vinegar
1/2 c. water
1/2 c. oil
2 c. sugar
1 t. celery seed
1 t. salt

Mix together all beans and vegetables in a large serving bowl; set aside.
In a separate bowl, whisk together remaining ingredients; toss with bean
mixture. Cover and refrigerate for at least 24 hours. Makes 10 to
12 servings.

53

Enjoy the coziness of your fireplace even when it's not in use. Set a
basket in the opening and fill it with lots of canning jars or milk bottles
overflowing with fresh flowers!

Mustard & Thyme Potato Salad

*This creamy potato salad is irresistible...you may want to
make a double batch!*

2 to 3 baking potatoes
1 to 2 T. red wine vinegar
1 c. mayonnaise
2 T. plus 2 t. Dijon mustard

1 t. fresh thyme, minced
pepper to taste
Garnish: additional fresh thyme

Pierce potatoes with a fork; bake at 400 degrees for 45 minutes, or until
tender. When potatoes are still warm but cool enough to handle, remove
and discard skins; cut into bite-size cubes. Transfer potatoes to a large bowl.
While potatoes are still warm, lightly drizzle with vinegar. Fold potatoes
over and lightly drizzle again. Gently fold once more; set aside. In a small
bowl, combine mayonnaise, mustard, thyme and pepper; pour over
potatoes. Fold until evenly coated. Transfer to a serving bowl; garnish with
thyme. Serve warm or chilled. Serves 4 to 6.

If you're turning on the oven to bake potatoes, why not bake a whole
oven full? You can grate them and dice them for hashbrowns, soups or
casseroles, slice them for home fries or whip up a quick potato salad!

Mustard & Thyme Potato Salad

Spinach & Clementine Salad

Spinach & Clementine Salad

This fresh, crunchy salad would be perfect for a summer picnic..

2 lbs. clementines, peeled
   and sectioned
2 lbs. baby spinach
4 stalks celery, thinly sliced on
   the diagonal
1 c. red onion, thinly sliced
1/2 c. pine nuts or walnuts,
   toasted

1/4 c. dried cherries
2 T. red wine vinegar
1/4 c. olive oil
1 t. Dijon mustard
1 clove garlic, minced
1/8 t. sugar
salt and pepper to taste

In a large salad bowl, combine clementines, spinach, celery, onion, nuts and cherries. Toss to mix well. Whisk together remaining ingredients in a small bowl; drizzle over salad. Serve immediately. Makes 8 servings.

Candied Pecans

These should be called Magical Pecans...they disappear right before your very eyes! Delicious on salads too.

1 t. cold water
1 egg white
1 lb. pecan halves

1 c. sugar
1 t. cinnamon
1/2 t. salt

In a large bowl, whisk together water and egg white until frothy; add pecans and mix well. In a small bowl, combine sugar, cinnamon and salt; mix well with pecans. Spread pecans on a greased baking sheet. Bake at 225 degrees for one hour, stirring occasionally. Cool completely; store in an airtight container. Makes one pound.

Summer in a Bowl

Summer in a Bowl

Do you have a backyard garden? This salad will make excellent use of all those peppers, cucumbers and tomatoes.

4 roma tomatoes, seeded and
 chopped
1 cubanelle pepper, seeded and
 chopped
1 cucumber, chopped
1/4 c. red onion, minced

6 fresh basil leaves, shredded
salt and pepper to taste
4 c. Italian bread, sliced, toasted
 and cubed
3 T. olive oil

Combine vegetables, basil, salt and pepper in a salad bowl. Let stand at room temperature for 30 minutes. At serving time, stir in bread cubes; drizzle with oil. Toss thoroughly; serve at room temperature. Serves 4.

There is no need for hurry in life...least of all when we are eating.
-Edward Everett Hale

Lemon-Dill Chopped Salad

Lemon-Dill Chopped Salad

Looking for fresh new salad ideas? You'll love this salad with its zesty homemade dressing.

2 romaine lettuce hearts, chopped
1 c. cherry tomatoes, quartered
1 cucumber, peeled and cubed
3/4 c. baby carrots, sliced into 1/4-inch coins
1/2 c. crumbled feta cheese

In a large bowl, combine lettuce, tomatoes, cucumber, carrots and cheese. Cover and refrigerate. At serving time, toss with Dressing. Serves 4.

Dressing:

juice of 1 lemon
2 T. white wine vinegar
1 T. honey
2 T. fresh dill, chopped
1/4 t. salt
1/8 t. pepper
1/3 c. olive oil
1 apple, cored and coarsely grated

Whisk together lemon juice, vinegar, honey, dill, salt and pepper. Slowly whisk in oil in a thin stream; stir in apple. Cover and refrigerate at least 2 hours.

If you bought a bunch of fresh herbs for a recipe that calls for just a couple of tablespoons, chop the extra herbs and add to a tossed salad. Fresh parsley, mint, dill, chives and basil all add extra flavor to salads.

Roasted Veggie Tortellini Salad

Roasted Veggie Tortellini Salad

Bored with the same old pasta salad? This bowlful of goodness is a must for any gathering!

20-oz. pkg. refrigerated 6-cheese
   tortellini pasta, uncooked
1 red pepper, thinly sliced
3/4 c. red onion, thinly sliced
1/2 lb. asparagus, trimmed and cut
   into 1-1/2 inch pieces

salt and pepper to taste
2 T. olive oil, divided
1 zucchini, diced
7-oz. container basil pesto sauce

Cook pasta according to package directions; drain, rinse with cold water and set aside. In a bowl, combine red pepper, onion and asparagus. Season with salt and pepper; toss with one tablespoon olive oil. Spread red pepper mixture in a single layer on a baking sheet. Bake at 450 degrees for 10 to 12 minutes. Remove from baking sheet; set aside. Season zucchini with salt and pepper; toss with remaining olive oil. Arrange in a single layer on baking sheet. Bake for 5 to 7 minutes, until tender and golden. Combine roasted vegetables, cooked tortellini and pesto in a large bowl. Chill for at least one hour; serve chilled. Makes 8 servings.

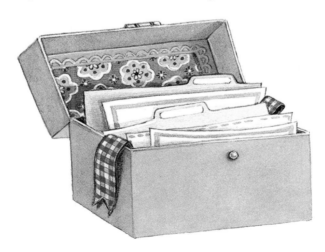

For hearty salads in a snap, keep cans of diced tomatoes, black olives, white beans and marinated artichoke hearts in the fridge. They'll be chilled and ready to toss with fresh greens at a moment's notice.

Invite your friends and neighbors to a good old-fashioned block party. Set up picnic tables, arrange lots of chairs in the shade and invite everyone to bring a favorite dish. Whether it's a summer cookout or a fall harvest party, you'll make some wonderful memories together!

Turn your favorite shredded pork, beef or chicken barbecue recipe into a delicious appetizer...make bite-size sandwiches on slider buns.

Toss together a yummy snack mix in a jiffy! Mix equal amounts of sweetened dried cranberries, salted peanuts and chocolate chips...great for munching on a bike ride or a hike in the woods.

Pitch a tent in the backyard on a clear night so the kids can camp out, watch the stars, tell tall tales and play flashlight tag. What a way to make memories!

Soups, Sandwiches & Breads

Grandma's Chicken Noodle Soup

*A big pot of chill-chasing chicken noodle soup...
old-fashioned goodness in every spoonful!*

12 c. chicken broth
1-1/2 t. salt
1 t. poultry seasoning
1 c. celery, diced
1 c. onion, diced
1 c. carrot, peeled and diced

1/3 c. cornstarch
1/4 c. cold water
16-oz. pkg. thin egg noodles,
 uncooked
4 c. cooked chicken, diced

Combine broth, salt and seasoning in a large soup pot; bring to a boil
over medium heat. Stir in vegetables; reduce heat to medium-low. Cover
and simmer for 15 minutes, stirring occasionally. Combine cornstarch and
cold water in a small bowl; gradually add to soup, stirring constantly.
Meanwhile, cook noodles according to package directions; drain. Stir
chicken and noodles into soup. Heat through, about 5 to 10 minutes.
Serves 8.

Cheer up an under-the-weather friend! Fill a fabric-lined basket
with homemade chicken soup, some hearty crackers, a big mug
and a cheerful book to read while recovering.

Grandma's Chicken Noodle Soup

Apple Jack Muffins

Soups, Sandwiches & Breads

Apple Jack Muffins

The best combination...apples and cinnamon!

2-1/3 c. all-purpose flour
1 c. sugar
2 t. cinnamon
1 T. baking powder
1 t. baking soda
1/2 t. salt
1-1/2 c. Granny Smith apples,
   peeled, cored and finely chopped

1 c. buttermilk
1/3 c. milk
1/3 c. ricotta cheese
3 T. oil
1 T. vanilla extract
2 egg whites, beaten
1 egg, beaten

In a large bowl, sift together flour, sugar, cinnamon, baking powder, baking soda and salt. Fold in apples; stir, then make a well in the center. In a separate bowl, whisk together remaining ingredients; pour into well in flour mixture. Gently stir until just moistened. Spoon batter into greased muffin cups, filling 2/3 full. Sprinkle Topping evenly over batter. Bake at 400 degrees for 18 minutes, or until a toothpick inserted in a muffin comes out clean. Makes 1-1/2 dozen.

Topping:

3 T. sugar

2 t. cinnamon

Combine ingredients in a cup.

Take time to share an icy glass of milk and a favorite treat with the kids after school...it's a great way to catch up and make sweet memories.

Homestyle Vegetable Soup

*Big bowls of this hearty country-style soup are sure
to satisfy on chilly days.*

3 to 3-1/2 lb. beef chuck roast
1 head cabbage, quartered
2 onions, chopped
4 15-oz. cans mixed vegetables

28-oz. can diced tomatoes
46-oz. can tomato juice
6-oz. can tomato paste
salt and pepper to taste

Place roast in an ungreased large roasting pan. Cover and bake at
325 degrees for 1-1/2 hours, until partially done. Add cabbage and onions
to pan; add enough water to cover. Cover and bake an additional one to
1-1/2 hours, until roast is very tender. Transfer contents of roasting pan to
a large soup pot. Stir in undrained vegetables, undrained tomatoes, tomato
juice, tomato paste, salt and pepper. Simmer over medium-low heat for one
to 1-1/2 hours, stirring often. At serving time, break up any large pieces
of roast. Makes 10 servings.

Italian Bean Soup

A hearty, filling soup that's ready to serve in a jiffy.

1 lb. ground pork sausage
1 onion, diced
1 clove garlic, minced
15-oz. can kidney beans, drained
and rinsed
15-oz. can black beans, drained
and rinsed

15-oz. can navy beans, drained
and rinsed
28-oz. can diced tomatoes
14-1/2 oz. can beef broth
2 T. grated Parmesan cheese
1 t. dried basil

Brown sausage with onion and garlic in a stockpot over medium heat;
drain. Stir in all beans, undrained tomatoes and remaining ingredients;
bring to a boil. Reduce heat to medium-low. Simmer for 15 to 20 minutes,
stirring occasionally. Serves 4 to 6.

Homestyle Vegetable Soup

Melt-In-Your-Mouth Biscuits

Melt-In-Your-Mouth Biscuits

*Split and served with butter and jam or honey, these flaky biscuits
live up to their name!*

1-1/2 c. all-purpose flour	1/4 c. chilled butter, sliced
1/2 c. whole-wheat flour	1/4 c. shortening
4 t. baking powder	2/3 c. milk
1/2 t. salt	1 egg, beaten
2 T. sugar	

In a large bowl, sift together flours, baking powder, salt and sugar; cut in
butter and shortening. Stir in milk and egg. Knead dough on a floured
surface until smooth; roll out to 1/2-inch thickness. Cut with a biscuit
cutter; place biscuits on ungreased baking sheets. Bake at 450 degrees for
10 to 15 minutes, until golden. Makes one to 2 dozen.

Buttery Farm Biscuits

*It isn't really a homestyle meal without a basket of hot biscuits,
straight from the oven!*

2 c. all-purpose flour	1/4 c. chilled butter, sliced
1 T. baking powder	3/4 c. milk
1/4 t. salt	

Combine flour, baking powder and salt in a large bowl; cut in butter with a
fork until mixture resembles coarse crumbs. Stir in milk until a soft dough
forms; roll into a large ball. Place dough on a lightly floured baking sheet;
flatten into a 9"x9" square. Cut dough into 12 square biscuits but do not
separate. Bake at 400 degrees for 15 to 20 minutes, until lightly golden.
Makes one dozen.

Sunday Meeting Tomato Soup

Fresh basil really makes this soup flavorful. Serve with grilled cheese sandwiches for a simply splendid lunch.

1/2 c. butter, sliced
1 c. fresh basil, chopped
2 cloves garlic, minced
2 28-oz. cans crushed tomatoes

1 qt. half-and-half
salt and pepper to taste
Garnish: shredded Parmesan
   cheese, herbed croutons

In a large saucepan, melt butter over medium heat. Add basil; sauté for 2 minutes. Add garlic and tomatoes with juice. Reduce heat to medium-low; simmer for 20 minutes, stirring occasionally. Remove from heat; let cool slightly. Working in batches, transfer tomato mixture to a blender and purée. Transfer back into saucepan and add half-and-half, mixing well. Reheat soup over low heat; season with salt and pepper. Ladle soup into bowls; garnish with cheese and croutons. Makes 8 to 10 servings.

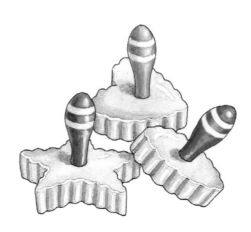

Top bowls of tomato soup with crunchy cheese toasts. Cut bread with a mini cookie cutter and brush lightly with olive oil. Place on a broiler pan and broil for 2 to 3 minutes, until golden. Turn over and sprinkle with freshly shredded Parmesan cheese. Broil another 2 to 3 minutes, until cheese melts.

Sunday Meeting Tomato Soup

Dilly Casserole Bread

Dilly Casserole Bread

There's nothing better than warm, fresh-baked bread! Even beginning bread bakers will find this recipe easy to make.

1 env. active dry yeast
1/4 c. warm water
1 c. cottage cheese
2 T. sugar
1 T. dried, minced onion
1/4 t. baking soda

1 egg, beaten
2 T. butter, softened and divided
2 t. dill weed, divided
1-1/2 t. salt, divided
2-1/4 to 2-1/2 c. all-purpose flour

Soften yeast in very warm water, about 110 to 115 degrees; set aside for 5 minutes. In a large bowl, combine cottage cheese, sugar, onion, baking soda, egg, one tablespoon butter, one teaspoon dill weed, one teaspoon salt and yeast mixture. Stir in enough flour to make a stiff dough. Cover and let rise until double in bulk, about 40 minutes. Stir dough down; place in a greased 9"x5" loaf pan. Let rise again for 40 minutes. Bake at 350 degrees for 35 to 40 minutes, until golden. Brush with remaining butter; sprinkle with remaining dill weed and salt. Makes one loaf.

77

A loaf of a favorite bread is such a thoughtful gift...
why not include the recipe along with a pretty vintage towel
tied with a bow?

Surprise Bean Soup

This creamy bean soup has something extra...peanut butter!

16-oz. pkg. bacon, cut into
   1-inch pieces
1 onion, chopped
1 c. carrot, peeled and diced
1 c. celery, chopped
15-oz. can tomato sauce

15-oz. can diced tomatoes
1 c. chicken broth
2 15-oz. cans navy beans, drained
3/4 c. creamy peanut butter
1/2 t. pepper

In a skillet over medium heat, cook bacon until crisp; drain. Return bacon to skillet; stir in onion, carrot and celery, cooking until onion is translucent. In a large stockpot over medium heat, stir together bacon mixture, tomato sauce, diced tomatoes, chicken broth and beans until hot and bubbly. Stir in peanut butter and pepper until well combined. Serve immediately. Makes 6 servings.

A quick & easy way to thicken bean soup...purée a cup of soup in a blender or mash it in a bowl, then stir it back into the soup pot.

Surprise Bean Soup

Granny's Country Cornbread

Granny's Country Cornbread

Pour the batter into vintage corn stick pans...the kids will love 'em!

1-1/4 c. cornmeal
3/4 c. all-purpose flour
5 T. sugar
2 t. baking powder
1/2 t. salt
1 c. buttermilk

1/3 c. oil
1 egg, beaten
1 c. shredded sharp Cheddar cheese
1 c. corn
1 T. jalapeño pepper, minced

Mix together cornmeal, flour, sugar, baking powder and salt in a large bowl. Make a well in center; pour in buttermilk, oil and egg. Stir just until ingredients are lightly moistened. Fold in cheese, corn and jalapeño; pour into a greased 8" cast-iron skillet. Bake at 375 degrees for 20 minutes, or until a tester inserted in the center comes out clean. Let cool slightly; cut into wedges. Makes 4 to 6 servings.

Mom's Sweet Potato Biscuits

Another delicious way to enjoy sweet potatoes.

2 c. self-rising flour
3 T. brown sugar, packed
1/4 t. cinnamon
1/8 t. allspice
3 T. shortening

1/4 c. plus 2 T. chilled butter, divided
1 c. canned sweet potatoes, drained and mashed
6 T. milk

Combine flour, brown sugar and spices in a large bowl; cut in shortening and 1/4 cup butter with a fork until crumbly. Add sweet potatoes and milk; stir just until moistened. Turn dough out onto a floured surface and knead several times. Roll out dough 1/2-inch thick; cut with a 2-inch round biscuit cutter. Place biscuits on an ungreased baking sheet. Melt remaining butter and brush over biscuits. Bake at 400 degrees for 10 to 12 minutes, until lightly golden. Makes about 1-1/2 dozen.

Chicken Corn Chowder Olé

An old favorite goes south of the border for a spicy new taste.

3 T. butter
1-1/2 lbs. boneless, skinless
   chicken breasts, cut into
   bite-size pieces
1/2 c. onion, chopped
1 to 2 cloves garlic, minced
2 cubes chicken bouillon
1 c. hot water

1/2 to 1 t. ground cumin
1 pt. half-and-half
8-oz. pkg. shredded Monterey
   Jack cheese
16-oz. can creamed corn
4-oz. can chopped green chiles
1/4 to 1 t. hot pepper sauce
1 tomato, diced

Melt butter in a Dutch oven over medium heat. Add chicken, onion and garlic; cook until chicken is no longer pink. Dissolve bouillon in hot water; add to chicken mixture. Stir in cumin; bring to a boil. Reduce heat; cover and simmer for 5 to 10 minutes. Add half-and-half, cheese, corn, chiles and hot sauce. Cook and stir over low heat until cheese is melted. Stir in tomato; serve immediately. Makes 6 to 8 servings.

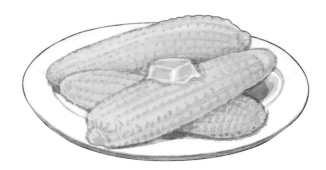

Keep in mind if half-and-half isn't in the fridge, an equal amount of evaporated milk can be substituted.

Chicken Corn Chowder Olé

Pioneer Beef Stew

Soups, Sandwiches & Breads

Pioneer Beef Stew

This delicious stew is baked, not simmered on the stovetop, so there's no need to watch it. Just right for an easy weekend!

14-1/2 oz. can petite diced
  tomatoes
1 c. water
3 T. quick-cooking tapioca,
  uncooked
2 t. sugar
1-1/2 t. salt
1/2 t. pepper
1-1/2 lbs. stew beef cubes
3 to 4 potatoes, peeled and cubed
4 carrots, peeled and thickly sliced
1 onion, diced

In a greased 3-quart casserole dish, combine tomatoes with juice, water, tapioca, sugar, salt and pepper. Mix well; gently stir in beef and vegetables. Cover and bake at 375 degrees for 1-1/2 to 2 hours, until beef and vegetables are tender. Serves 4 to 6.

Beef Stew & Biscuits

There's nothing more satisfying than a hearty bowl of beef stew! This tried & true one-pot meal is perfect for Sunday dinner.

1 lb. ground beef
1/4 c. onion, chopped
3-1/2 c. frozen mixed vegetables,
  thawed
2 8-oz. cans tomato sauce
1/4 t. dried basil
1/8 t. pepper
1 c. sharp Cheddar cheese, cubed
12-oz. tube refrigerated biscuits

In a large skillet over medium heat, brown beef and onion; drain. Add vegetables, tomato sauce and seasonings; mix well. Cover and simmer for 5 minutes. Fold in cheese cubes; pour into a lightly greased 2-quart casserole dish. Arrange biscuits on top. Bake, uncovered, at 375 degrees for 25 minutes, or until bubbly and biscuits are golden. Serves 4 to 6.

Baked Potato Soup

Mmm...is there anything more satisfying than a steamy bowl of potato soup on a chilly day? We don't think so!

10 slices bacon, diced
3 c. potatoes, peeled and cubed
14-1/2 oz. can chicken broth
1 carrot, peeled and grated
1/2 c. onion, chopped
1 T. dried parsley
1/2 t. celery seed
1/2 t. salt
1/2 t. pepper
3 T. all-purpose flour
3 c. milk
1/4 lb. pasteurized process cheese
   spread, cubed
Garnish: thinly sliced green onions

In a large soup pot, cook bacon until crisp; drain and crumble bacon. Set aside 1/3 of bacon; return remaining bacon to soup pot. Add potatoes, broth, carrot, onion and seasonings. Cover and simmer until potatoes are tender, stirring occasionally, about 15 minutes. In a bowl, whisk together flour and milk until smooth; add to soup. Bring to a boil; cook and stir for 2 minutes. Add cheese; stir until cheese melts. Ladle soup into bowls; garnish with green onions and reserved bacon. Serves 8.

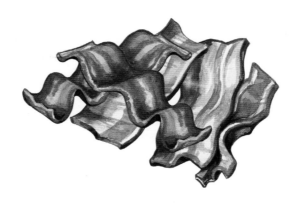

Prepare crispy bacon easily for topping soups and sandwiches. Place bacon slices on a broiler pan. Bake at 400 degrees for 12 to 15 minutes. Turn bacon over and bake for another 8 to 10 minutes.

Baked Potato Soup

Cornmeal-Cheddar Biscuits

Cornmeal-Cheddar Biscuits

*If you're a real Cheddar fan, try making these biscuits
with extra-sharp Cheddar cheese!*

1-1/2 c. all-purpose flour
1/2 c. yellow cornmeal
2 t. sugar
1 T. baking powder

1/4 to 1/2 t. salt
1/2 c. butter, softened
1/2 c. shredded Cheddar cheese
1 c. milk

In a bowl, combine flour, cornmeal, sugar, baking powder and salt. Cut in butter with a fork until mixture resembles coarse crumbs. Stir in cheese and milk just until moistened. Drop dough by 1/4 cupfuls onto an ungreased baking sheet. Bake at 450 degrees for 12 to 15 minutes, until lightly golden. Serve warm. Makes one dozen.

A single vintage quilt patch makes a charming topper for a bread basket...just stitch it to a large napkin in a matching color.

Great American Submarine

*This oversize sandwich is picnic-perfect...gather your friends
and enjoy a warm day in the country!*

1-lb. loaf Italian bread
1/2 c. mayonnaise
1/2 lb. deli honey ham,
  thinly sliced
1/2 lb. deli salami, thinly sliced
1 tomato, thinly sliced
1 onion, thinly sliced
1 green pepper, thinly sliced
  into rings

1/2 lb. Muenster cheese, sliced
2 3.8-oz. cans sliced black olives,
  drained
2 banana peppers, seeded and
  sliced
1 bunch leaf lettuce, torn
salt and pepper to taste

Slice loaf in half horizontally. Spread cut side of bottom half with
mayonnaise. Layer remaining ingredients in order given; top with
remaining half of loaf. Slice and serve, or wrap well in plastic wrap and
tuck in a picnic cooler. Makes 4 servings.

Invite everyone to a soup & sandwich party...perfect for game day!
With a big pot of your heartiest soup, freshly made sub sandwiches
and brownies for dessert, you'll all have time to relax
and enjoy the game.

Great American Submarine

Cheeseburger Roll-Ups

Cheeseburger Roll-Ups

*A fun and different way to enjoy everybody's favorite cheeseburgers...
great for block parties!*

2 lbs. ground beef
3/4 c. soft bread crumbs
1/2 c. onion, minced
2 eggs, beaten
1-1/2 t. salt

1-1/2 t. pepper
12-oz. pkg. shredded Cheddar
  cheese
6 to 8 sandwich buns, split
Garnish: catsup, mustard, lettuce

In a large bowl, combine beef, bread crumbs, onion, eggs, salt and pepper;
mix well using your hands. Pat out on a piece of wax paper into an 18-inch
by 14-inch rectangle. Spread cheese over beef mixture, leaving a 3/4-inch
border around edges. Roll up jelly-roll fashion, starting at one short edge.
Press ends to seal. Place on a lightly greased 15"x10" jelly-roll pan. Bake at
350 degrees for one hour, or until internal temperature on a meat
thermometer reaches 160 degrees. Let stand at least 10 minutes before
slicing. Slice and serve on buns; garnish as desired. Serves 6 to 8.

For zesty French fries that are anything but boring,
spray frozen fries with non-stick olive oil spray and sprinkle
with your favorite spice blend like Italian, Cajun or steak
seasoning. Spread on a baking sheet and bake as directed.

Tex-Mex Meatball Subs

Just for fun, serve sandwiches in paper napkin-lined baskets with tortilla chips and a dill pickle.

1-1/2 lbs. ground beef
1 egg, beaten
1 c. tortilla chips, crushed
1-1/4 oz. pkg. taco seasoning
  mix, divided
16-oz. jar salsa, divided

26-oz. jar spaghetti sauce
8 hoagie or sub buns, split
1/2 lb. Monterey Jack cheese,
  sliced
Optional: lettuce leaves, sliced
  jalapeño peppers

Mix together beef, egg, crushed chips, half of taco seasoning and one cup salsa. Form into one-inch balls; place in an ungreased 13"x9" baking pan. Bake, uncovered, at 375 degrees for 45 minutes; remove from oven and drain. Combine sauce, remaining salsa and remaining seasoning in a saucepan. Simmer for several minutes over low heat; pour over meatballs. Spoon meatballs and sauce onto buns; top with cheese slices. Garnish with lettuce and jalapeños, if desired. Makes 8 sandwiches.

94

Refrigerator Pickles

Super simple...a great recipe for first-time pickle makers.

3 c. cucumbers, peeled
  and sliced
1 onion, thinly sliced
3/4 c. sugar

2/3 c. white vinegar
1/2 t. celery seed
1/2 t. mustard seed
1/4 t. salt

Combine cucumbers and onion in a large glass jar or bowl; set aside. Stir together remaining ingredients in a microwave-safe container. Microwave on high for 3 minutes, stirring after 2 minutes. Pour over cucumber mixture. Cover and refrigerate for 24 hours before serving to blend flavors. Keep refrigerated. Makes one quart.

Tex-Mex Meatball Subs

Chili & Biscuits

Chili & Biscuits

Two family favorites combined into one easy dinner! If time is short, you can bake the biscuits separately while the chili is simmering.

1 lb. ground beef
1 onion, chopped
4 stalks celery, chopped
1-1/4 oz. pkg. chili seasoning mix
1/4 c. all-purpose flour
28-oz. can diced tomatoes

15-1/2 oz. can chili beans
Optional: 4-oz. can sliced
   mushrooms, drained
garlic powder, salt and pepper
   to taste

In a large skillet over medium heat, brown together beef, onion and celery; drain. Stir in chili seasoning and flour; add remaining ingredients. Reduce heat to medium-low. Simmer until thickened and bubbly, about 15 minutes, stirring often. Transfer chili to a lightly greased 13"x9" baking pan. Drop Biscuit Dough by tablespoonfuls over top. Bake, uncovered, at 375 degrees for 10 to 15 minutes, until biscuits are golden. Serves 6 to 8.

Biscuit Dough:

1-1/2 c. all-purpose flour
1 c. yellow cornmeal
2 T. sugar
4 t. baking powder

1/2 t. salt
1/2 c. oil
1/2 to 3/4 c. milk

Combine dry ingredients and oil. Stir in enough milk to form a soft dough.

A chili cook-off! Ask neighbors to bring a pot of their best "secret recipe" chili to share, then have a friendly judging for the best. You provide lots of crackers and buttered cornbread, cool drinks and bright red bandannas for terrific lap-size napkins.

So-Easy Pork Fritters

These tasty fritters are excellent in sandwiches...they're delicious served with mashed potatoes and gravy too.

1 lb. pork tenderloin, sliced
   1/2-inch thick
1 egg, beaten
3 T. milk
1 sleeve saltine crackers, finely
   crushed

3/4 c. all-purpose flour
1 t. salt
1/2 t. pepper
oil for frying
Optional: 4 sandwich buns,
    lettuce, tomato slices

Place pork slices between 2 pieces of wax paper. Using a rolling pin, flatten to 1/4-inch thickness; set aside. Whisk together egg and milk in a small bowl. Combine cracker crumbs, flour and seasonings in a separate bowl. Dip pork slices into egg mixture, then press in crumb mixture until well coated. Heat 1/2 inch oil in a skillet over medium-high heat. Add pork slices; fry until deep golden on both sides and no longer pink in the middle, turning as needed. If desired, serve fritters in buns, topped with lettuce and tomatoes. Makes 4 servings.

A handy all-purpose seasoning to keep by the stove! Simply mix 6 tablespoons salt and one tablespoon pepper and fill a large shaker. It's just right for sprinkling on pork chops, burgers, chicken and homestyle potatoes.

So-Easy Pork Fritters

Baked Filled Sandwiches

Baked Filled Sandwiches

This dish will wow 'em at parties...warm bread, melty cheese,
tender ham and turkey all in one.

1 loaf frozen bread dough, thawed
2 T. mayonnaise-type salad
   dressing
1-1/2 t. dried, minced onion
3/4 t. Italian seasoning
8 slices Swiss cheese

10 slices deli honey ham
10 slices deli roast turkey
1 egg, beaten
1 t. water
Garnish: sesame seed

On a floured surface, roll dough into a 14-inch by 12-inch rectangle.
Spread with salad dressing; sprinkle with onion and seasoning. Make ten,
1-1/2 inch cuts on each long edge of the dough. Layer center of dough
alternately with cheese, ham and turkey slices, ending with turkey.
Criss-cross the cut strips over the top; place on an ungreased baking sheet.
Combine egg and water; brush over dough. Sprinkle with sesame seed;
let rise for 30 minutes. Bake at 350 degrees for 45 minutes to one hour,
until golden. Slice to serve. Serves 8.

101

A cut-to-size length of linen or medium-weave burlap
makes a great no-sew tablecloth. To add fringe,
just pull away threads, one row at a time.

Pizza Bread Twists

Refrigerated pizza dough lets you twist up these tasty sticks in a jiffy!
Serve them alongside soup or add to an appetizer buffet.

1/2 c. sun-dried tomatoes in oil,
   drained and finely chopped
4 t. olive oil
4 t. water
1/2 c. grated Parmesan cheese

3/4 t. dried oregano
1/4 t. pepper
2 10-oz. tubes refrigerated pizza
   dough, divided

In a bowl, whisk together all ingredients except dough; set aside. Unroll one tube of dough on a lightly floured surface; pat or roll into a 10-inch by 8-inch rectangle. Spread half of tomato mixture over dough; fold dough in half crosswise. Slice dough lengthwise into ten strips, each 1/2-inch wide. Twist each strip 2 to 3 times; place on a lightly greased baking sheet. Repeat with remaining dough and tomato mixture. Bake at 350 degrees for 12 to 15 minutes, until golden. Cool on a wire rack. Makes about 1-1/2 dozen.

For a quick and casual centerpiece, curl a string of
dried chile peppers into a circle, then set a hurricane
with a fat red candle in the center.

Pizza Bread Twists

Hot Chicken Sandwiches

Hot Chicken Sandwiches

An old midwestern favorite that's often found at hometown barn sale and ball game concessions.

6-oz. pkg. chicken-flavored
  stuffing mix
6-oz. pkg. herb-flavored stuffing
  mix
12-1/2 oz. can chicken, drained
  and flaked

10-3/4 oz. can cream of chicken
  soup
sandwich buns, split

In a stockpot, prepare stuffing mixes as packages direct. Mix in chicken and soup. Increase heat to medium; cook and stir until heated through. Serve on buns. Serves 8 to 10.

Simply Coleslaw

Pineapple and carrots give this coleslaw a pleasing sweetness.

1 head cabbage, chopped
  or shredded
4 carrots, peeled and grated
8-oz. can crushed pineapple,
  drained

1 onion, chopped
1 c. plain yogurt
salt and pepper to taste
Optional: garlic powder and
  paprika to taste

In a large serving bowl, mix cabbage, carrots, pineapple, onion and yogurt. Season with salt and pepper to taste. If desired, add garlic powder and paprika. Cover and chill for 30 minutes before serving. Serves 6 to 8.

Buffalo Chicken Sandwich

This delicious sandwich is very easy to make. Sure to become your go-to recipe when friends are coming for a casual meal.

6 boneless, skinless
  chicken breasts
1 onion, chopped
6 stalks celery, chopped
2 to 3 T. olive oil
1/2 c. all-purpose flour
Optional: 1 t. seasoning salt

17-1/2 oz. bottle buffalo
  wing sauce
6 soft buns, split
Garnish: ranch or blue cheese salad
  dressing, crumbled blue cheese,
  additional wing sauce

Flatten chicken breasts to 1/4-inch thin between pieces of wax paper; set aside. In a skillet over medium-low heat, sauté onion and celery in oil until tender. In a shallow bowl, combine flour and seasoning salt, if using. Dredge chicken pieces in flour mixture. Add chicken on top of onion mixture in pan. Cook for 5 minutes; flip chicken and cook an additional 5 minutes. Add buffalo wing sauce to pan. Cover; increase heat to medium, and cook 5 to 7 minutes, until chicken juices run clear. Serve on buns; garnish as desired. Makes 6 sandwiches.

Sandwich buns just taste better toasted...they won't get soggy either. Simply butter buns lightly and place on a hot grill for 30 seconds to one minute, until toasted to taste.

Buffalo Chicken Sandwich

Chicken Enchilada Soup

This recipe may seem lengthy, but it goes together in a jiffy! Serve it with a simple salad of ripe tomato and avocado drizzled with lime vinaigrette dressing.

1 onion, chopped
1 clove garlic, pressed
1 to 2 t. oil
14-1/2 oz. can chicken broth
14-1/2 oz. can beef broth
10-3/4 oz. can cream of chicken soup
1-1/2 c. water
13-oz. can chicken, drained

4-oz. can chopped green chiles
2 t. Worcestershire sauce
1 T. steak sauce
1 t. ground cumin
1 t. chili powder
1/8 t. pepper
6 corn tortillas, cut into strips
1 c. shredded Cheddar cheese

In a stockpot over medium heat, sauté onion and garlic in oil. Add remaining ingredients except tortilla strips and cheese; bring to a boil. Cover; reduce heat and simmer for one hour, stirring occasionally. Uncover; stir in tortilla strips and cheese. Simmer an additional 10 minutes. Serves 6.

Welcoming extra guests for dinner? It's easy to stretch a pot of soup to make more servings...just add an extra can or two of tomatoes or beans. The soup will be extra hearty, and no one will know the difference!

Chicken Enchilada Soup

Hearty Sausage Soup

On chilly nights, this soup will become a family favorite! Vary it by using part hot sausage along with the Kielbasa.

1 T. olive oil
3 lbs. Kielbasa sausage, cut into
  bite-size pieces
3 onions, diced
3 cloves garlic, minced
3 16-oz. cans kidney beans,
  drained and rinsed
3 14-1/2 oz. cans diced tomatoes,
  drained

14-1/2 oz. can beef broth
1/2 c. long-cooking rice, uncooked
0.67-oz. pkg. fresh basil, chopped
1 t. Italian seasoning
1 t. dried oregano
1 t. dried parsley

Heat oil in a large stockpot over medium heat. Add Kielbasa, onions and garlic. Cook until golden; drain. Add remaining ingredients; bring to a boil over medium-high heat. Reduce heat to low; simmer for 1-1/2 hours, stirring occasionally. Add a little water, as needed. Makes 8 to 10 servings.

Make your own flavorful vegetable broth. Coarsely chop 3 celery stalks with leaves, 2 or 3 large carrots, a large onion and several cloves of garlic. It's not necessary to peel the veggies. Place them in a soup pot and cover with water. Bring to a boil, then reduce heat. Simmer gently for an hour; strain. Broth may be used right away or frozen to use later.

Hearty Sausage Soup

Soup is sure to be even tastier served up in toasty bread bowls. Slice the tops off bread rounds, scoop out and spritz with non-stick olive oil spray. Sprinkle with Italian seasoning and grated Parmesan cheese, if you like. Bake for about 10 minutes at 350 degrees.

Pull out your oversize coffee mugs when serving soups, stews and chili. They're just right for sharing hearty servings, and the handles make them so easy to hold onto.

Give tonight's table a little flair...knot a cheery bandanna around each set of flatware. Bandannas come in so many bright colors, everyone can choose their own favorite.

Make the most of leftover slices of country-style bread...turn them into crispy croutons for soups and salads! Toss bread cubes with olive oil and chopped herbs. Toast on a baking sheet at 400 degrees for 5 to 10 minutes, until golden.

Slow-Cooker Favorites

Bacon-Horseradish Dip

Put a slow cooker to work cooking up this creamy,
cheesy dip...it's irresistible!

3 8-oz. pkgs. cream cheese,
   softened
12-oz. pkg. shredded Cheddar
   cheese
1 c. half-and-half
1/3 c. green onions, chopped
3 cloves garlic, minced

3 T. prepared horseradish
1 T. Worcestershire sauce
1/2 t. pepper
12 slices bacon, crisply cooked
   and crumbled
bagel chips or assorted crackers

Combine all ingredients except bacon and chips or crackers in a slow cooker. Cover and cook on low setting for 4 to 5 hours, or on high setting for 2 to 2-1/2 hours, stirring once halfway through cooking time. Just before serving, stir in bacon. Serve with bagel chips or crackers. Makes 7 to 8 cups.

114

Make your own toasty baguette chips to serve with dips and spreads. Thinly slice a loaf of French bread. Brush slices with olive oil; place on a baking sheet and sprinkle with grated Parmesan cheese. Bake at 350 degrees until crisp and golden, about 10 minutes.

Bacon-Horseradish Dip

Chipotle-Black Bean Dip

Chipotle-Black Bean Dip

*This smoky, spicy bean dip is sure to be the hit
at your next tailgating party!*

16-oz. can refried beans
15-oz. can black beans, drained
  and rinsed
11-oz. can sweet corn & diced
  peppers, drained
1 c. chunky salsa
1-1/2 c. shredded Cheddar cheese,
  divided

2 chipotle chiles in adobo sauce,
  chopped and 2 t. adobo sauce
  reserved
Garnish: chopped green onions
tortilla chips

Mix together beans, corn, salsa, one cup cheese, chiles and reserved adobo
sauce in a slow cooker. Cover and cook on low setting for 3 to 4 hours,
stirring after 2 hours. Sprinkle with remaining cheese; garnish with green
onions. Serve with tortilla chips. Makes 12 servings.

117

Hosting a get-together? Use slow cookers set on low to keep creamy dips
and saucy finger foods warm and toasty.

Cranberry Kielbasa Bites

Need a new idea for harvest get-togethers? Try this scrumptious recipe...friends won't believe it when you tell them what's in it!

2 16-oz. Kielbasa sausage rings, cut into 1/2-inch pieces
2 14-oz. pkgs. mini smoked sausages
3/4 c. catsup
14-oz. can whole-berry cranberry sauce
1/2 c. grape jelly

Combine all ingredients in a slow cooker; stir to mix well. Cover and cook on low setting for 7 to 8 hours. Serves 10 to 12.

Honey Sesame Wings

Sweet and tangy, but not too spicy. You'll love them!

3 lbs. chicken wings, cut into sections
salt and pepper to taste
2 c. honey
1 c. soy sauce
1/2 c. catsup
1/4 c. oil
2 cloves garlic, minced
Garnish: sesame seed

Place chicken wings on an ungreased broiler pan; sprinkle with salt and pepper. Place pan 4 to 5 inches under broiler. Broil for about 10 minutes on each side, until golden. Transfer wings to a slow cooker. Combine remaining ingredients except sesame seed; spoon over wings. Cover and cook on low setting for 4 to 5 hours. Arrange wings on a serving platter; sprinkle with sesame seed. Makes about 2-1/2 dozen.

Cranberry Kielbasa Bites

Susan's Slow-Cookin' Ribs

Susan's Slow-Cookin' Ribs

These ribs melt in your mouth! Serve them as is,
or shredded and used for sandwiches.

1 T. onion powder
1 t. red pepper flakes
1/2 t. dry mustard
1/2 t. garlic powder
1/2 t. allspice
1/2 t. cinnamon
3 lbs. boneless pork ribs, sliced
   into serving-size pieces and
   divided

1 onion, sliced and divided
1/2 c. water
2 c. hickory-flavored barbecue
   sauce

Combine seasonings in a cup; mix well and rub over ribs. Arrange 1/3 of ribs in a slow cooker; top with 1/3 of onion slices. Repeat layering 2 more times, ending with onion. Pour water over all. Cover and cook on low setting for 8 to 10 hours. Drain and discard liquid from slow cooker. Pour barbecue sauce over ribs. Cover and cook on low setting for an additional one to 2 hours. Serves 6 to 8.

121

Juicy BBQ sandwiches are best served on a vintage-style
oilcloth...saucy spills wipe right up! Look for one with
a colorful design of fruit or flowers.

Italian Meatball Subs

These meatballs are so good, you'll want to make a double batch and freeze half for another meal! They're delicious over pasta too.

1 lb. ground beef
1 c. Italian-seasoned dry
   bread crumbs
1/2 c. grated Parmesan cheese
1 T. fresh parsley, minced
1 clove garlic, minced
1/2 c. milk

1 egg, beaten
1-1/2 t. salt
1/2 t. pepper
8 sub buns, split
Garnish: shredded mozzarella
   cheese

Combine uncooked beef and remaining ingredients except buns and mozzarella cheese in a large bowl; mix well with your hands. Form into 2-inch balls; place in a slow cooker. Spoon Chunky Tomato Sauce over meatballs. Cover and cook on low setting for 8 to 9 hours. Place 3 to 4 meatballs on each bun; top with sauce and cheese. Makes 8 servings.

Chunky Tomato Sauce:

28-oz. can tomato purée
28-oz. can Italian-style crushed
   tomatoes
1/2 c. grated Parmesan cheese

2 1-1/2 oz. pkgs. spaghetti
   sauce mix
salt and pepper to taste

Mix all ingredients in a saucepan over medium heat; simmer until well blended.

Make mealtime extra special with cloth napkins. Glue wooden alphabet letter initials to plain napkin rings, one for each family member.

Italian Meatball Subs

Slow-Cooker Sloppy Joes

Slow-Cooker Sloppy Joes

Start this in the morning, then relax...
dinner will be ready when you are!

1-1/2 lbs. ground beef
1 c. onion, diced
2 cloves garlic, minced
1/2 c. green pepper, diced
1/2 c. celery, diced
3/4 c. catsup
1/4 c. water

1 T. brown sugar, packed
2 T. vinegar
2 T. Worcestershire sauce
2 T. mustard
1-1/2 t. chili powder
6 to 8 hamburger buns, toasted
Optional: pickle slices

In a skillet over medium heat, brown beef, onion and garlic; drain and set aside. In a slow cooker, combine remaining ingredients except buns and pickles; stir in beef mixture. Cover and cook on low setting for 6 to 8 hours. Spoon onto buns; garnish with pickle slices, if desired. Serves 6 to 8.

Slow-Cooker Cheesesteak Sandwiches

125

Slow-roasted flavor with very little effort! Freeze the beef
for a few minutes first...slicing will be a snap.

1 lb. beef round steak, thinly sliced
1/2 onion, diced
1 red pepper, diced
1-1/2 t. garlic powder
1 T. butter

1 T. Worcestershire sauce
1 cube beef bouillon
16-oz. pkg. shredded Colby Jack
   cheese
4 hoagie rolls, split

Combine all ingredients except cheese and rolls in a lightly greased slow cooker. Add enough water to just cover the ingredients. Cover and cook on low setting for 6 to 8 hours, until beef is tender. Using a slotted spoon, place a serving of steak mixture on the bottom half of each roll. Sprinkle with cheese; replace top halves of rolls. Makes 4 sandwiches.

Chicken Taco Soup

A spicy and flavorful soup...serve this favorite with bandannas
for napkins and a bottle of hot pepper sauce for those who like it fiery!

1 onion, chopped
16-oz. can chili beans
15-oz. can black beans
15-oz. can corn
2 10-oz. cans diced tomatoes
   with green chiles
1-1/2 c. chicken broth

8-oz. can tomato sauce
1-1/4 oz. pkg. taco seasoning mix
3 boneless, skinless chicken
   breasts
Garnish: shredded Cheddar cheese,
   crushed tortilla chips, sour
   cream

In a slow cooker, mix together onion, beans, corn, diced tomatoes with juice, chicken broth and tomato sauce. Do not drain beans or vegetables. Add seasoning mix; stir to blend. Lightly press chicken breasts into mixture until partially covered. Cover and cook on low setting for 5 hours, or until chicken is tender. Remove chicken from slow cooker; shred and return to soup. Cover and cook for an additional 2 hours. Top servings with cheese, crushed chips and sour cream, as desired. Serves 8.

Crunchy tortilla strips are a tasty addition to southwestern-style soups.
Cut corn tortillas into thin strips, then deep-fry quickly. Drain on paper
towels before sprinkling over bowls of soup. Try red or blue tortilla
chips just for fun!

Chicken Taco Soup

Turkey & Wild Rice Soup

Turkey & Wild Rice Soup

This hearty soup is chock-full of veggies! It's a perfect way to turn leftover Thanksgiving turkey into a completely different meal too.

1/2 c. onion, chopped
2 t. oil
1 c. deli smoked turkey, diced
1 c. celery, diced
1 c. carrots, peeled and diced
1/2 c. long-cooking wild rice, uncooked
1 t. dried tarragon
1/4 t. pepper
2 14-oz. cans regular or low-sodium chicken broth
12-oz. can regular or fat-free evaporated milk
1/3 c. all-purpose flour
1 c. frozen peas, thawed

In a skillet over medium heat, sauté onion in oil until tender, about 4 minutes. In a slow cooker, combine onion mixture, turkey, celery, carrots, rice and seasonings; stir in broth. Cover and cook on low setting for 6 to 8 hours. About 30 minutes before serving time, mix evaporated milk and flour; stir into soup along with peas. Cover and cook on low setting for about 20 minutes, until thickened. Makes 6 servings.

129

A trip to the pick-your-own farm and a haywagon ride in the countryside are sure to stir up appetites. Come home to a hearty slow-cooked dinner that's ready when you are!

Squash, Chickpea & Lentil Stew

*This colorful stew is healthy and hearty...fill up your slow cooker,
then work up an appetite with a with a hike in the woods!*

3/4 c. dried chickpeas or
   garbanzo beans
2-1/2 lbs. butternut squash, peeled
   and cut into 1/2-inch cubes
2 carrots, peeled and sliced
1 onion, chopped
1 c. dried lentils
4 c. vegetable broth

2 T. tomato paste
1 T. fresh ginger, peeled and grated
1-1/2 t. ground cumin
1 t. salt
1/4 t. pepper
1/4 c. lime juice
Garnish: chopped peanuts, chopped
   fresh cilantro

Cover chickpeas with 2 inches of water; let soak overnight. Drain chickpeas;
combine with remaining ingredients except lime juice and garnish in a slow
cooker. Cover and cook on low setting for 5 to 6 hours. Stir in lime juice;
sprinkle servings with peanuts and cilantro. Serves 8.

Keep frozen chopped onions, peppers and veggie blends on hand for
quick slow-cooker meal prep. They'll thaw quickly so you can toss
together a recipe in a snap...no peeling, chopping or dicing.

Squash, Chickpea & Lentil Stew

Country Chicken Stew

Country Chicken Stew

A savory, filling meal in a bowl. Garnish with shredded Monterey Jack cheese and diced avocado, if you like.

4 boneless, skinless chicken thighs
3-1/2 c. chicken broth
2 c. roma tomatoes, chopped
1 c. green pepper, chopped
1 c. onion, chopped
1/2 c. long-cooking rice, uncooked

1/2 c. canned garbanzo beans, drained and rinsed
3 cloves garlic, chopped
1/2 t. salt
1/2 t. pepper
1 bay leaf

Combine all ingredients except garnish in a slow cooker. Cover and cook on low setting for 7 to 9 hours, until chicken and rice are tender. Discard bay leaf. To serve, place a piece of chicken in each soup bowl; ladle stew over chicken. Serves 4.

Brunswick Stew

There's old-fashioned flavor in every spoonful of this hearty stew.

133

3-lb. boneless pork shoulder roast, quartered
3 redskin potatoes, diced
1 onion, chopped
28-oz. can crushed tomatoes
18-oz. bottle favorite barbecue sauce

14-oz. can chicken broth
9-oz. pkg. frozen baby lima beans, thawed
9-oz. pkg. frozen corn, thawed
6 T. brown sugar, packed
1 t. salt

Stir together all ingredients in a slow cooker. Cover and cook on low setting for 6 hours, or until pork and potatoes are tender. Remove pork with a slotted spoon; shred. Return pork to slow cooker; stir well. Ladle stew into bowls. Serves 8.

Chicken Stuffing Casserole

*Hearty and so filling, this midwestern favorite will be
the first to disappear at any potluck.*

12-oz. pkg. chicken-flavored
  stuffing mix
3 10-3/4 oz. cans cream of
  chicken soup, divided
1/2 c. milk
3 to 4 c. cooked chicken, cubed
12-oz. pkg. shredded Cheddar
  cheese

Prepare stuffing mix according to package directions; spoon into a slow
cooker. Stir in 2 cans soup. In a separate bowl, stir together remaining soup,
milk and chicken; add to slow cooker. Spread cheese over top. Cover and
cook on low setting for 4 to 6 hours, or on high setting for 2 to 3 hours.
Serves 6.

Potlucks are so easy...everyone brings along their favorite dish to share.
Why not plan a casual get-together with friends? It's all about food
and fellowship!

Chicken Stuffing Casserole

Too-Easy Roast Chicken

Too-Easy Roast Chicken

Like store-bought rotisserie chicken, but better! Serve it up for dinner with all the trimmings, or shred and use in all your favorite recipes.

2 t. kosher salt
1 t. paprika
1 t. onion powder
1 t. Italian seasoning
1/2 t. dried thyme
1/2 t. pepper

1/2 t. cayenne pepper
1/8 t. chili powder
4 to 5-lb. roasting chicken
4 cloves garlic
1 onion, quartered

Combine spices in a cup; mix well and rub over all sides of chicken. Place chicken, breast-side down, in a large slow cooker. Put garlic and onion inside chicken cavity. Cover and cook on low setting for 8 to 10 hours, until juices run clear. Serves 4 to 6.

Southern Green Beans & Potatoes

A meal in itself with a pan of cornbread...serve alongside ham or pork chops for a real country-style dinner.

137

6 slices bacon, cut into 1-inch
  pieces and partially cooked
4 to 6 redskin potatoes, thinly
  sliced
4 to 5 c. green beans, trimmed

10-3/4 oz. can cream of celery
  soup
2 T. dried, minced onion
salt and pepper to taste

Combine all ingredients in a large slow cooker; stir gently. Cover and cook on low setting for 7 to 9 hours. Serves 4 to 6.

Pot Roast & Dumplings

This is one of our favorite meals on a chilly day...at the end of a busy day, dinner is practically ready!

5 potatoes, peeled and halved
2 c. baby carrots
4-lb. beef chuck roast

garlic salt and pepper to taste
2 c. water
1-oz. pkg. onion soup mix

Place potatoes and carrots in a large slow cooker. Place roast on top; sprinkle with seasonings. Stir together water and soup mix; pour over roast. Cover and cook on low setting for 6 to 8 hours, until roast is tender. Drain most of the broth from slow cooker into a large soup pot; bring to a boil over medium-high heat. Drop teaspoonfuls of batter for Dumplings into boiling broth. Cover and cook for 15 minutes. Serve roast with vegetables and dumplings. Makes 8 to 10 servings.

Dumplings:

2 c. all-purpose flour
3 T. baking powder

1/2 t. salt
1 c. light cream

Mix together flour, baking powder and salt. Add cream; stir quickly to make a medium-soft batter.

Alongside each slow cooker, use alphabet game pieces to spell out soup names. Guests will know just what's inside and it's a fun twist on the traditional table tent.

Pot Roast & Dumplings

Mom's Classic Cabbage Rolls

Mom's Classic Cabbage Rolls

Simple and delicious, especially good on a cool autumn day.

1-1/2 lbs. ground beef
1/2 c. instant rice, uncooked
1 egg, beaten
1 t. garlic powder

1/2 t. salt
1/2 t. pepper
1 onion, diced
12 to 14 cabbage leaves

In a bowl, combine uncooked beef and remaining ingredients except cabbage leaves; mix well and set aside. Drop cabbage leaves into boiling water for 3 to 4 minutes, until pliable; drain. Place 1/4 cup beef mixture in the center of each leaf. Fold in sides and roll up; set aside. Pour half the Tomato Sauce into a slow cooker; arrange cabbage rolls over sauce. Pour remaining sauce over rolls. Cover and cook on high setting for 5 to 6 hours. Serves 4 to 6.

Tomato Sauce:

2 8-oz. cans tomato sauce
juice of 2 lemons

3 T. all-purpose flour
1/2 c. sugar

141

Combine all ingredients in a bowl; mix well.

A hearty slow-cooked dish is perfect on a sunny evening. Carry the crock right out to your backyard picnic table and savor the fresh air with your family!

Smoky Hobo Dinner

An old camping favorite...now it can be enjoyed on rainy days too!

5 potatoes, peeled and quartered
1 head cabbage, coarsely chopped
16-oz. pkg. baby carrots
1 onion, thickly sliced

salt and pepper to taste
16-oz. pkg. smoked pork sausage,
 sliced into 2-inch pieces
1/2 c. water

Spray a slow cooker with non-stick vegetable spray. Layer vegetables in slow cooker in order listed, sprinkling each layer with salt and pepper. Place sausage on top of vegetables; pour water into slow cooker. Cover and cook on low setting for 6 to 8 hours. Serves 6.

Camp-Out Chili Dogs

*Great for tailgating, or a take-it-easy meal for
a lazy day with the kids.*

1 lb. hot dogs
2 15-oz. cans chili with beans
1 onion, finely chopped

1 t. chili powder
1 c. shredded Cheddar cheese
8 hot dog rolls, split

Place hot dogs in a slow cooker. In a bowl, combine chili, onion and chili powder; stir well and pour over hot dogs. Cover and cook on low setting for 4 to 6 hours, or on high setting for 1-1/2 to 2 hours. Add cheese just before serving; allow to melt slightly. Serve each hot dog in a roll with some chili spooned over top. Serves 6 to 8.

Smoky Hobo Dinner

Apple Butter BBQ Spareribs

Apple Butter BBQ Spareribs

*Theses ribs taste amazing! For another delicious way, try this
same recipe using a pork roast and add apricot preserves
in place of the apple butter.*

4 lbs. pork spareribs
salt and pepper to taste
16-oz. jar apple butter

18-oz. bottle barbecue sauce
1 onion, quartered

Season ribs with salt and pepper; place ribs on rimmed baking sheets. Bake
at 350 degrees for 30 minutes; drain. Meanwhile, blend together apple
butter and barbecue sauce in a bowl; set aside. Cut ribs into serving-size
pieces and place in a slow cooker. Top ribs with onion; drizzle sauce mixture
over all. Cover and cook on low setting for 8 hours, until ribs are very
tender. Makes 4 to 6 servings.

Use your garden's bounty to create a colorful centerpiece. Squash,
peppers, eggplant, onions and shallots are beautiful piled in baskets
and country containers. Later, you can use the veggies in soups
and casseroles.

Calico Beans

No family reunion spread is complete without a big crock
of these sweet and savory beans.

2 lbs. ground beef, browned
   and drained
1/2 to 1 lb. bacon, crisply cooked
   and crumbled
1 onion, chopped
3 15-oz. cans pork & beans
2 16-oz. cans kidney beans

2 16-oz. cans baby butter beans
16-oz. can navy beans
1 c. catsup
1/2 c. brown sugar, packed
2 T. prepared horseradish
2 T. Worcestershire sauce
hot pepper sauce to taste

Add all ingredients to a slow cooker; do not drain beans. Stir well. Cover and cook on low setting for 6 hours. Stir again before serving. Serves 20.

Treat yourself to a quick getaway on a sunny day! Check out some nearby places you've always wanted to see...gardens, craft shops, historic houses. Pack a picnic lunch and stop at a park you've never visited before. Sure to be fun!

Calico Beans

Deliciously Cheesy Potatoes

Deliciously Cheesy Potatoes

An old favorite...perfect alongside baked ham, barbecue ribs or even at brunch.

32-oz. pkg. frozen southern-style hashbrowns, thawed
2 10-3/4 oz. cans Cheddar cheese soup
2 12-oz. cans evaporated milk
2 2.8-oz. cans French fried onions, divided

In a large bowl, combine hashbrowns, soup and milk. Spoon half of mixture into a slow cooker; top with one can of onions. Add remaining potato mixture; top with remaining onions. Cover and cook on low setting for 8 hours, stirring occasionally. Serves 8 to 10.

Buttery Acorn Squash

Raisins, brown sugar and pumpkin pie spice...a scrumptious harvest time recipe.

3/4 c. brown sugar, packed
2 t. pumpkin pie spice
2 acorn squash, halved and seeded
3/4 c. raisins
1/4 c. butter, sliced
1/2 c. water

In a small bowl, combine brown sugar and spice; spoon into squash halves. Sprinkle with raisins; dot with butter. Wrap each squash half separately in heavy-duty aluminum foil; seal tightly. Add water to a slow cooker. Place squash in slow cooker, cut-side up, stacking packets if necessary. Cover and cook on high setting for 4 hours, until squash is tender. Open packets carefully to allow steam to escape. Makes 4 servings.

Country-Style Bread Pudding

This is the best-tasting bread pudding ever, and so much easier than making it in the oven. Family & friends will love it!

3/4 c. brown sugar, packed
8 slices cinnamon-raisin bread
3 to 4 T. butter, softened
4 eggs, beaten

3-1/2 c. milk
1-1/2 t. vanilla extract
Garnish: whipped cream

Spray a slow cooker with non-stick vegetable spray. Sprinkle brown sugar into slow cooker; set aside. Spread bread slices with butter; cube bread and add to slow cooker. Whisk together remaining ingredients except whipped cream; pour over bread. Cover and cook on high setting for 2 to 3 hours, until thickened. Do not stir. Spoon warm pudding into dessert bowls. Drizzle with brown sugar sauce from the slow cooker; garnish with whipped cream. Makes 8 to 10 servings.

Dollop fresh whipped cream on homestyle desserts...irresistible!
Pour a pint of whipping cream into a deep, narrow bowl. Beat with
an electric mixer on medium speed, gradually increasing to
high speed. When soft peaks form, add sugar to taste.

Country-Style Bread Pudding

Praline Apple Crisp

Slow-Cooker Favorites

Praline Apple Crisp

What's more comforting than warm apple crisp? This old-fashioned dessert is sure to be welcomed at potlucks and get-togethers of all kinds.

6 Granny Smith apples, peeled,
   cored and sliced
1 t. cinnamon
1/2 c. quick-cooking oats,
   uncooked
1/3 c. brown sugar, packed
1/4 c. all-purpose flour
1/2 c. chilled butter, diced
1/2 c. chopped pecans
1/2 c. toffee baking bits
Optional: whipped cream

Toss together apples and cinnamon in a large bowl. Place in a slow cooker sprayed with non-stick vegetable spray; set aside. In a separate bowl, combine oats, brown sugar, flour and butter; mix with a fork until crumbly. Stir in pecans and toffee bits; sprinkle over apples. Cover and cook on low setting for 4 to 6 hours, until apples are tender. Top with whipped cream, if desired. Makes 10 servings.

Triple Chocolate Cake

This ooey-gooey dessert is a chocolate lover's delight!

18-1/2 oz. pkg. chocolate cake mix
8-oz. container sour cream
3.9-oz. pkg. instant chocolate
   pudding mix
12-oz. pkg. semi-sweet chocolate
   chips
4 eggs, beaten
3/4 c. oil
1 c. water
Garnish: vanilla ice cream

Place all ingredients except ice cream in a slow cooker; mix well. Cover and cook on high setting for 3 to 4 hours. Serve warm, garnished with scoops of ice cream. Makes 8 to 10 servings.

Hot Spicy Cider for a Crowd

*A crock-full of hot cider to sip...your secret to
keeping warm on blustery days.*

1 gal. apple cider
1 c. sugar
2 t. ground cloves
2 t. allspice

2 4-inch cinnamon sticks
1/4 c. orange juice
Optional: apple wedges

Combine all ingredients except apples in a slow cooker. Cover and cook on low setting for 5 to 6 hours, or on high setting for 2 to 3 hours. Discard cinnamon sticks before serving. Garnish individual servings with apple wedges, if desired. Makes about one gallon.

A collection of coffee mugs is fun for serving hot beverages to a crowd!
Pick up one-of-a-kind novelty or souvenir mugs for a song at yard sales.

Hot Spicy Cider for a Crowd

Bayou Chicken

You'll love the combination of slow-cooked flavors in this recipe.

3 boneless, skinless chicken
   breasts, cubed
14-1/2 oz. can chicken broth
14-1/2 oz. can diced tomatoes
10-3/4 oz. can tomato soup
1/2 lb. Kielbasa sausage, sliced

1/2 c. cooked ham, diced
1 onion, chopped
2 t. Cajun seasoning
hot pepper sauce to taste
cooked rice

In a slow cooker, combine all ingredients except rice; stir gently. Cover and cook on low setting for 6 to 8 hours. To serve, ladle over cooked rice. Serves 6 to 8.

Give chicken thighs a try in slow-cooker chicken recipes. They're often priced lower than chicken breasts, and the darker meat cooks up juicy and flavorful. You may find you like them best!

Bayou Chicken

Hearty Hominy Beef Stew

Sliced avocado makes a delicious garnish for this unusual stew.

1 onion, chopped
2-lb. beef chuck roast, cubed
1/4 t. salt
1 green pepper, chopped
3 carrots, peeled and sliced
3 stalks celery, sliced
3 cloves garlic, minced

14-1/2 oz. can petite diced
  tomatoes
1 c. beef broth, divided
2 T. cornstarch
15-oz. can hominy, drained and
  rinsed
Optional: sliced avocado

Place onion in a slow cooker; top with beef. Sprinkle with salt. Add green pepper, carrots, celery and garlic to slow cooker. Pour tomatoes with juice and 3/4 cup broth over all. Cover and cook on low setting for 7 to 8 hours. In a bowl, mix together cornstarch and remaining broth until smooth; stir into slow cooker during the last 15 minutes of cooking time. Stir in hominy and heat through. Garnish as desired. Serves 6.

Slow cookers are a super budget helper! Cheaper cuts of beef like round steak and chuck roast cook up fork-tender, juicy and flavorful...there's simply no need to purchase more expensive cuts.

Hearty Hominy Beef Stew

Easy Chili Rellenos

A potluck pleaser that's welcome almost any time of day.

2 t. butter
7-oz. can whole green chiles,
   drained and cut into strips
8-oz. pkg. shredded Cheddar
   cheese
8-oz. pkg. shredded Monterey Jack
   cheese

14-1/2 oz. can stewed tomatoes
4 eggs, beaten
2 T. all-purpose flour
3/4 c. evaporated milk

Spread butter in a slow cooker. Arrange chiles in a single layer; top with cheeses. Pour tomatoes with juice over cheeses. In a bowl, whisk together eggs, flour and milk; pour into slow cooker. Cover and cook on high setting for 2 to 3 hours. Serves 6.

A tasty side for any south-of-the-border main dish...stir salsa and shredded cheese into hot cooked rice. Cover and let stand a few minutes, until cheese melts...olé!

Easy Chili Rellenos

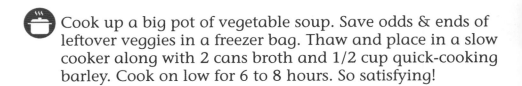 Cook up a big pot of vegetable soup. Save odds & ends of leftover veggies in a freezer bag. Thaw and place in a slow cooker along with 2 cans broth and 1/2 cup quick-cooking barley. Cook on low for 6 to 8 hours. So satisfying!

Simple slow-cooker recipes are ideal for older children just learning to cook. With supervision, they can learn to use paring knives, can openers and hot mitts...and they'll be proud to serve the dinner they've prepared!

If a favorite recipe calls for cooking on the stovetop for a long, low simmer, it can usually be converted to a slow-cooker recipe. Two to 4 hours of stovetop or oven cooking time will convert to 4 to 6 hours on the high setting of the slow cooker, or 7 to 9 hours on the low setting.

Slow-cooker gravy...it's a must with mashed potatoes! Remove your roast beef or chicken to a platter, leaving the juices in the slow cooker. Make a smooth paste of 1/4 cup flour or cornstarch and 1/4 cup cold water. Pour into the slow cooker and stir well. Turn the cooker to the high setting and cook for 15 minutes once the mixture comes to a boil.

Mains &
Side Dishes

Hearty Chicken Pie

This country-style pie is a real crowd-pleaser! Whether served at a social event or at home, it's always the first dish to disappear.

4 c. cooked chicken, cubed
10-3/4 oz. can cream of chicken
  soup
10-1/2 oz. can chicken broth
1/2 t. poultry seasoning

16-oz. can sliced carrots, drained
1-1/2 c. all-purpose flour
2 t. baking powder
1-1/2 c. buttermilk
1/2 c. butter, melted

Place chicken in a lightly greased 13"x9" baking pan. Combine soup, broth and seasoning in a bowl; spoon over chicken. Arrange carrots on top. In a separate bowl, mix together flour and baking powder; stir in buttermilk and melted butter until smooth. Spoon batter over carrots. Bake, uncovered, at 350 degrees for one hour, or until bubbly and crust is golden. Serves 6.

Old-Fashioned Creamed Corn

This is the best creamed corn you'll ever taste! After harvest time, this is a great use for the corn you've put away in the freezer... you'll need about three cups of kernels.

6 ears sweet corn, husked
1/4 c. bacon drippings
1/4 c. water

2 T. all-purpose flour
1/2 c. milk
sugar, salt and pepper to taste

Remove kernels from corn, reserving as much liquid as possible; set aside. Heat drippings in a cast-iron skillet over medium heat. Add corn, reserved liquid and water; cook for 15 minutes. In a cup, whisk flour into milk; slowly add to corn. Reduce heat to low and cook, stirring frequently, until mixture thickens. Sprinkle with sugar, salt and pepper; stir to blend. Makes 6 servings.

Hearty Chicken Pie

Garden Skillet Dinner

Garden Skillet Dinner

One-pot comfort food at its finest...warm chicken and vegetables with noodles. Clean-up is quick as a wink!

12-oz. pkg. medium egg noodles, uncooked
1 lb. boneless, skinless chicken breasts, cubed
1/4 c. all-purpose flour
1/3 c. olive oil
2 T. garlic, minced
1 T. dried basil
1/2 c. red pepper, sliced
1/2 c. carrot, peeled and sliced
1/2 c. celery, sliced
1/2 c. broccoli flowerets
3/4 c. chicken broth
3/4 c. whipping cream
salt and pepper to taste

Cook noodles according to package directions; drain. Meanwhile, combine chicken and flour in a large plastic zipping bag. Seal bag and shake until chicken is evenly coated; discard remaining flour. Heat oil in a large skillet over medium heat. Sauté chicken in oil until golden and no longer pink in the center. Add garlic, basil and vegetables to skillet; cook for 2 minutes. Reduce heat to low; stir in broth and cream. When mixture has thickened slightly, stir in cooked noodles. Heat through; season with salt and pepper. Serves 4 to 6.

167

A simple green salad goes well with all kinds of hearty main dishes. For a zesty lemon dressing, shake up 1/2 cup olive oil, 1/3 cup fresh lemon juice and a tablespoon of Dijon mustard in a small jar and chill to blend.

Herb Garden Turkey Breast

You'll be proud to serve this savory, juicy turkey to holiday guests...
so much easier than roasting a whole bird.

8-1/2 lb. turkey breast, thawed
   if frozen
3 T. lemon juice, divided
2 T. oil, divided
2 cloves garlic, minced

1 t. lemon zest
2 t. fresh thyme, chopped
1 t. fresh sage, chopped
1-1/4 t. salt
3/4 t. pepper

Place turkey breast on a rack in an ungreased shallow roasting pan; loosen skin on top without removing it. Combine one tablespoon lemon juice, one tablespoon oil, garlic, lemon zest and seasonings; spread under loosened skin. Combine remaining lemon juice and oil; set aside. Bake, uncovered, at 350 degrees for 2-1/2 to 3 hours, basting every 15 to 20 minutes with reserved lemon juice mixture. Turkey is done when a meat thermometer inserted into thickest part reads 165 degrees. Remove to a serving platter; let stand for 10 minutes before slicing. Makes 14 to 16 servings.

168

Do you have lots of leftover turkey? It freezes well up to 3 months. Cut turkey into bite-size pieces, place in plastic freezer bags and pop in the freezer...ready to stir into hearty casseroles or soups.

Herb Garden Turkey Breast

Fluffy French Bread Stuffing

Fluffy French Bread Stuffing

*Your family is sure to love this sage-flavored stuffing...
you may want to make two batches!*

8 c. soft French bread, cubed
1 c. saltine crackers, crushed
1 t. dried sage
1 c. onion, chopped
1/2 c. celery, chopped

1/2 c. butter, sliced
10-3/4 oz. can cream of
    chicken soup
2 eggs, beaten
1/4 c. fresh parsley, chopped

Combine bread cubes, cracker crumbs and sage in a large bowl; set aside.
In a skillet over medium heat, cook onion and celery in butter until tender.
Spoon onion mixture over bread mixture. Add soup, eggs and parsley; toss
lightly. Transfer mixture to a lightly greased 4-quart casserole dish. Cover
with aluminum foil; bake at 350 degrees for one hour. May also be used
to stuff a 6 to 8-pound turkey or two, 3 to 4-pound chickens. Makes
8 servings.

171

Day-old bread is fine for making stuffing cubes, croutons and
casserole toppings. It keeps its texture better than very
fresh bread...it's budget-friendly too.

Ham & Cauliflower Au Gratin

Moms, you're sure to love this yummy recipe...kids will eat their veggies without complaining!

2 10-oz. pkgs. frozen cauliflower, thawed and drained
1-1/4 c. smoked ham, diced
10-3/4 oz. can Cheddar cheese soup
1/4 c. milk
2/3 c. biscuit baking mix
2 to 3 T. butter, softened
1/2 t. nutmeg
dried parsley and paprika to taste

Arrange cauliflower in a lightly greased 13"x9" baking pan; sprinkle with ham. Whisk together soup and milk until smooth; pour over top. Toss together biscuit mix, butter and nutmeg with a fork until crumbly; sprinkle over soup mixture. Sprinkle with parsley and paprika. Bake, uncovered, at 400 degrees until cauliflower is tender and topping is golden, 20 to 25 minutes. Makes 6 to 8 servings.

172

Broccoli & Cheese Squares

Perfect for potlucks...even broccoli haters will love this cheesy broccoli dish!

3 T. butter, melted
3 eggs
1 c. milk
1 c. all-purpose flour
1 t. baking powder
1 t. salt
3 8-oz. pkgs. shredded mild Cheddar cheese
2 10-oz. pkgs. frozen chopped broccoli, cooked and drained
2 t. onion, chopped

Spread melted butter in the bottom of a 13"x9" baking pan; set aside. Beat eggs in a large bowl. Add milk, flour, baking powder and salt; mix well. Stir in cheese, broccoli and onion; spoon into pan. Bake, uncovered, at 350 degrees until set, 30 to 35 minutes. Cut into squares. Serves 8 to 10.

Ham & Cauliflower Au Gratin

Famous White Mac & Cheese

Famous White Mac & Cheese

Real homemade mac & cheese...just like Mom used to make!
Sure to put a smile on everyone's face.

16-oz. pkg. elbow macaroni,
   uncooked
2 T. butter
2 T. all-purpose flour

3 c. milk
1 lb. Monterey Jack cheese, cubed
1/2 lb. Pepper Jack cheese, cubed

Cook macaroni according to package directions; drain and set aside.
Meanwhile, melt butter in a saucepan over medium heat. Stir in flour until
combined; add milk and stir until mixture boils. Remove from heat; add
cheese and stir until melted. Combine cheese mixture and cooked macaroni;
place in an ungreased 13"x9" baking pan. Bake, uncovered, at 350 degrees
for 30 minutes, or until bubbly. Makes 8 servings.

175

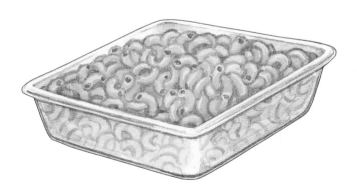

Wrap and freeze small amounts of leftover cheeses.
They may become crumbly when thawed, but will
still be delicious in baked dishes.

Baked Steak with Gravy

Juicy and tender, yet easy on the wallet, this steak is drenched in the easiest gravy ever.

1 c. all-purpose flour
1/8 t. salt
1/8 t. pepper
6 to 8 beef cube steaks
1 T. butter

2 10-3/4 oz. cans golden
    mushroom soup
2-1/2 c. water
4-oz. can sliced mushrooms,
    drained

Mix flour, salt and pepper in a shallow bowl. Dredge steaks in flour mixture and set aside. Melt butter in a large skillet over medium heat. Add steaks and brown on both sides, working in batches if necessary. Arrange steaks in a lightly greased 13"x9" baking pan. Combine soup, water and mushrooms in a bowl; spoon soup mixture over steaks. Cover with aluminum foil; bake at 325 degrees for 45 to 50 minutes. Uncover; bake an additional 15 minutes. Serves 6 to 8.

Mashed potatoes are the perfect partner for Baked Steak with Gravy. Make 'em in a jiffy! Cut peeled potatoes into quarters and cook in boiling water until tender, 15 to 18 minutes. Drain, mash right in the pot and stir in butter, salt and a little milk to desired consistency.

Baked Steak with Gravy

Cheddar Potato Gratin

Cheddar Potato Gratin

*Everyone's favorite cheesy potatoes...especially scrumptious
with baked ham.*

2 t. dried sage
1-1/2 t. salt
1/2 t. pepper
3 lbs. potatoes, peeled, thinly sliced
  and divided

1 onion, thinly sliced and divided
8-oz. pkg. shredded Cheddar
  cheese, divided
1 c. whipping cream
1 c. chicken broth

Mix sage, salt and pepper in a cup; set aside. Layer 1/3 of potatoes and half
of onion in a lightly greased 13"x9" baking pan. Sprinkle with one
teaspoon of sage mixture and 1/3 of cheese. Repeat layers with remaining
ingredients, ending with cheese. Whisk cream and broth together until well
blended; pour evenly over top. Bake, covered, at 400 degrees for one hour,
until tender and golden. Let stand 5 minutes before serving. Makes 10 to
12 servings.

179

Cran-Orange Pork Medallions

Ready in just 30 minutes...what a time-saver!

1 to 1-1/2 lb. pork tenderloin,
  cut into 1-inch slices
1/2 t. garlic powder
1/2 t. coriander
1/2 t. salt
1/4 t. pepper

2 T. olive oil
1 red onion, chopped
1/2 c. orange marmalade
1/4 c. orange juice
1/4 c. sweetened dried cranberries
2 T. balsamic vinegar

Place pork slices between 2 pieces of wax paper. Using a rolling pin, flatten to 1/4-inch thickness. Combine seasonings; sprinkle over both sides of pork. In a large skillet over medium heat, sauté pork in oil for 3 minutes on each side, or until juices run clear. Remove and keep warm. In same skillet, sauté onion in pan juices for 5 minutes, or until tender. Stir in remaining ingredients; bring to a boil. Reduce heat; return pork to skillet. Simmer, uncovered, for 5 minutes, or until sauce is thickened. Serve medallions topped with sauce from skillet. Makes 4 servings.

Steam vegetables to keep their fresh-picked taste...it's simple. Bring 1/2 inch of water to a boil in a saucepan and add cut-up veggies. Cover and cook to desired tenderness, about 3 to 5 minutes. A quick toss with a little butter and they're ready to enjoy.

Cran-Orange Pork Medallions

Harvest Casserole

Harvest Casserole

*Packed full of wonderful vegetables grown in your own backyard
or from the nearest farmers' market...you'll savor every bite.*

1/2 c. long-cooking rice, uncooked
4 redskin potatoes, cut into thin
   wedges
1/4 c. butter, sliced and divided
1 T. fresh sage, chopped

3 red peppers, chopped
1 onion, sliced
2 zucchini, thinly sliced
1 c. shredded Cheddar cheese

Cook rice according to package directions. Meanwhile, arrange potatoes in
a greased 2-1/2 quart casserole dish; dot with half the butter. Layer with
half each of the sage, red peppers, onion, zucchini and cooked rice. Repeat
layers; cover with aluminum foil. Bake at 350 degrees for one hour, or until
potatoes are tender. Uncover; sprinkle cheese over top and return to oven
until cheese is melted, about 5 minutes. Serves 6.

Dust off Mom's vintage casserole dishes...they're just right
for baking family-pleasing hearty casseroles, with a
side dish of sweet memories.

Easy Skillet Lasagna

Delicious and simple to make, with this lasagna you won't even have to heat up the oven on a warm day.

6 lasagna noodles, uncooked
1 lb. ground beef or turkey
1 onion, finely chopped
1/2 c. green pepper, finely chopped
1 clove garlic, minced
24-oz. jar spaghetti sauce

12-oz. container small-curd cottage cheese, divided
4 slices mozzarella cheese, divided
1/2 c. grated Parmesan cheese, divided

Cook noodles according to package directions; drain and cut noodles in half. Meanwhile, in a skillet over medium heat, brown beef with onion, green pepper and garlic; drain. Transfer beef mixture to a bowl; stir in spaghetti sauce. In same skillet, layer 1/3 of beef mixture and half each of the noodles and cheeses. Repeat layers. Top with remaining beef mixture, making sure to cover all noodles. Cover and simmer over medium-low heat for 10 to 15 minutes. Remove from heat. Let stand for 10 minutes before uncovering and serving. Serves 4.

For flavorful, fast-fix garlic bread, brush Italian bread slices with softened butter. Sprinkle on garlic & herb seasoning blend and broil until golden.

Easy Skillet Lasagna

Penne with Sausage & Cheese

Penne with Sausage & Cheese

Everybody loves this cheesy pasta casserole! It's just right for family dinners...carry-ins and potlucks too.

12-oz. pkg. penne pasta, uncooked
1 lb. hot or mild Italian ground
   pork sausage
3 cloves garlic, chopped
26-oz. jar tomato & basil
   spaghetti sauce

1/2 t. red pepper flakes
1/2 t. salt
1/2 t. pepper
1 c. shredded mozzarella cheese
Garnish: grated Parmesan cheese,
   chopped fresh parsley

Cook pasta according to package directions; drain. Meanwhile, in a skillet over medium heat, cook sausage until browned; drain. Add garlic and cook until tender, about 2 minutes. Stir in sauce and seasonings. Stir sauce mixture into cooked pasta; transfer mixture to a greased 12"x8" baking pan. Top with mozzarella cheese. Bake, covered, at 375 degrees for 25 to 30 minutes, until bubbly and cheese is melted. Sprinkle with Parmesan cheese and parsley. Makes 6 servings.

187

Pasta shapes like bowties, seashells, wagon wheels and corkscrew-shaped cavatappi all work well in casseroles... why not give a favorite casserole a whole new look?

Company Green Beans

A green bean casserole that's a little different...
even vegetable haters will love it!

3 slices bacon
1/4 c. red onion, finely grated
2 t. garlic, minced
2 14-1/2 oz. cans French-style
  green beans, drained

1 tomato, chopped
salt and pepper to taste
1/2 c. shredded sharp Cheddar
  cheese

In a skillet over medium heat, cook bacon until crisp. Drain bacon and crumble, reserving drippings in skillet. Add onion and garlic to reserved drippings; cook until slightly softened. Remove from heat; stir in beans, tomato and seasonings. Transfer mixture to a greased 8"x8" baking pan and sprinkle with cheese. Bake, covered, at 400 degrees for 15 minutes. Uncover; reduce heat to 350 degrees and bake an additional 5 to 10 minutes. Serves 4 to 6.

188

Wild Rice Bake

A savory side dish that's ready to bake in a jiffy. Slip it
into the oven alongside a roast.

2 10-3/4 oz. cans French onion
  soup
2 10-1/2 oz. cans beef broth
2 8-oz. cans sliced water
  chestnuts, drained
8-oz. can sliced mushrooms,
  drained

6-oz. pkg. long grain & wild
  rice with seasoning packet,
  uncooked
1 c. butter, diced

In an ungreased 13"x9" baking pan, combine all ingredients including contents of seasoning packet. Stir gently to mix. Cover and bake for one hour at 350 degrees. Serves 6 to 8.

Company Green Beans

Hamburger Noodle Casserole

Hamburger Noodle Casserole

*This quick & easy recipe uses basic ingredients,
comes together in a snap and tastes so good.*

16-oz. pkg. wide egg noodles,
  uncooked
1-3/4 lbs. lean ground beef
1 onion, chopped
1 green pepper, chopped
1 t. salt
1 t. pepper
26-oz. can cream of mushroom
  soup
12-oz. pkg. shredded Cheddar
  cheese

Cook noodles according to package directions; drain. Meanwhile, in a skillet over medium heat, brown beef with onion and green pepper. Drain; season with salt and pepper. Combine cooked noodles, beef mixture and soup; stir gently to mix. Transfer to a greased 13"x9" baking pan; top with cheese. Bake, uncovered, at 325 degrees for 10 to 15 minutes, until bubbly and cheese is melted. Serves 6 to 8.

191

Even the simplest meal is special when shared. Why not invite a dinner guest or two the next time you have a tasty dinner in the oven? The menu doesn't need to be fancy...it's sure to be appreciated!

Tangy Corn Casserole

A great side dish for celebrations or even for brunch.

10-oz. pkg. frozen corn, thawed
  and drained
1/2 c. onion, chopped
1/2 c. green pepper, sliced
1/2 c. water
1 c. yellow squash, chopped
1 tomato, chopped
1 c. shredded Cheddar cheese,
  divided

2/3 c. cornmeal
1/2 c. milk
2 eggs, beaten
3/4 t. salt
1/4 t. pepper
1/4 t. hot pepper sauce

In a saucepan over medium heat, combine corn, onion, green pepper and water; bring to a boil. Reduce heat to medium-low; cover and simmer 5 minutes. Do not drain. In a bowl, combine squash, tomato, 3/4 cup cheese and remaining ingredients. Stir corn mixture into squash mixture. Transfer to a greased 1-1/2 quart casserole dish. Bake, uncovered, at 350 degrees for 45 to 50 minutes, until bubbly and golden. Top with remaining cheese. Serves 6 to 8.

192

Enjoy a taste of summer in fall...make an extra of
a favorite farm-fresh casserole to tuck into the freezer.
Wrap well with plastic wrap and freeze. To serve,
thaw overnight in the refrigerator and bake as usual.

Tangy Corn Casserole

Fire & Spice Baked Ham

Fire & Spice Baked Ham

*Is there anything more taste-tempting than the aroma
of a baked ham? We don't think so!*

5-1/2 to 6-lb. fully cooked
   ham half
1/2 c. red pepper jelly

1/2 c. pineapple preserves
1/4 c. brown sugar, packed
1/4 t. ground cloves

Trim off rind and excess fat from ham; score fat in a diamond pattern.
Place ham on a broiler pan sprayed with non-stick vegetable spray.
Combine remaining ingredients in a small saucepan over low heat, stirring
with a whisk until well blended. Brush 1/3 of jelly mixture over ham.
Bake, uncovered, at 425 degrees for 5 minutes. Reduce oven temperature
to 325 degrees. Bake ham for an additional 45 minutes, basting with
remaining jelly mixture every 15 minutes. Transfer ham to a serving platter;
let stand for 15 minutes before slicing. Makes 8 to 10 servings.

Cranberry Fruit Conserve

This colorful relish goes well with roast turkey, chicken and pork.

12-oz. pkg. fresh cranberries
1-3/4 c. sugar
1 c. water
1 Granny Smith apple, peeled,
   cored and diced

zest and juice of 1 orange
zest and juice of 1 lemon
3/4 c. golden raisins
3/4 c. chopped walnuts or pecans

In a saucepan, combine cranberries, sugar and water. Cook over medium-
low heat for 5 minutes, or until cranberries pop. Add apple, citrus zest and
juice; continue cooking over low heat for 15 minutes. Remove from heat;
stir in raisins and nuts. Cover and refrigerate; serve chilled. Makes about
5 cups.

Sweet Potato-Apple Bake

A really tasty change from the traditional sweet potato casseroles we're used to.

4 sweet potatoes, boiled, peeled and sliced
1/2 c. butter, sliced
1/2 c. sugar
1/2 c. brown sugar, packed
1 to 2 t. cinnamon

4 tart apples, peeled, cored and sliced
1/2 c. water
1/4 c. lemon juice
1/4 c. orange juice

Arrange a layer of sliced sweet potatoes in a greased one-quart casserole dish. Dot with butter; sprinkle with sugars and cinnamon. Arrange a layer of sliced apples on top; continue layering until all ingredients except water and juices are used. Combine water and juices; pour gently over top. Cover and bake at 400 degrees for 45 minutes, or until apples are tender. Makes 4 to 6 servings.

196

Keep a jar of pumpkin pie spice on hand in the kitchen. A blend of cinnamon, ginger, nutmeg and cloves, it's delicious on apples and sweet potatoes, not just baked goods!

Sweet Potato-Apple Bake

Campers' Beans

Campers' Beans

It wouldn't be a cookout without a pot of baked beans.
Sweet and satisfying, it's almost a meal in itself!

6 to 8 slices bacon
1 onion, chopped
1/4 c. brown sugar, packed
1/4 c. catsup
2 T. mustard

2 t. cider vinegar
2 32-oz. cans baked beans
Optional: additional crumbled
    bacon

Crisply cook bacon in a skillet over medium-high heat. When partially cooked, add onion; continue cooking until bacon is crisp. Drain bacon and onion on paper towels; crumble bacon. Combine brown sugar, catsup, mustard and vinegar in a large saucepan; simmer over low heat for 15 minutes. Stir in beans with liquid, bacon and onion. Simmer, uncovered, for at least 30 minutes, stirring occasionally. If desired, garnish with additional bacon. Makes 8 to 10 servings.

199

Prefer to use dried beans instead of canned? Dried beans can be slow-cooked for 8 hours to overnight on low. Cover with water and add a teaspoon of baking soda. In the morning, drain well and use immediately, or cover and refrigerate for up to 3 days.

Chicken Chestnut Casserole

A great make-ahead dish....real comfort food, and you don't even have to precook the macaroni!

6 boneless, skinless chicken
   breasts
1 t. salt
7-oz. pkg. elbow macaroni,
   uncooked
2 10-3/4 oz. cans cream of
   mushroom soup

1 c. milk
12-oz. pkg. shredded Cheddar
   cheese
8-oz. can sliced water chestnuts,
   drained
2-oz. jar diced pimentos, drained
1 onion, finely chopped

In a large saucepan, cover chicken with water; bring to a boil over medium-high heat. Stir in salt. Reduce heat to low and simmer just until chicken is tender, about 25 minutes. Drain, reserving 1-1/2 cups broth from the saucepan. Cube chicken; set aside. Mix reserved broth, uncooked macaroni and remaining ingredients in a large bowl. Fold in chicken; spread mixture in a lightly greased 13"x9" baking pan. Cover and refrigerate for at least 12 hours. Bake, uncovered, at 325 degrees for one hour and 15 minutes. Serves 8 to 10.

Dress up stemmed glasses in a jiffy. Cut or tear fabric into 1/2-inch wide strips and tie a length around the stem of the glass. Choose seasonal colors to match the occasion.

Chicken Chestnut Casserole

Roasted Citrus-Herb Salmon

Roasted Citrus-Herb Salmon

This delicious main dish is sure to be welcome whenever you're in the mood for a lighter meal.

2 to 3-lb. salmon fillet
1 T. fresh parsley, chopped
1 T. fresh thyme, chopped
1 T. garlic, minced
1 T. olive oil

2 t. lemon zest
2 t. lime zest
1-1/2 t. salt
1/2 t. pepper

Arrange salmon on a parchment paper-lined baking sheet. Combine remaining ingredients in a small bowl; spread herb mixture over salmon. Bake, uncovered, at 400 degrees for 12 to 15 minutes, until salmon flakes easily with a fork. Serves 4 to 6.

A pat of herb butter makes delicious food taste even better. Simply blend chopped fresh herbs into softened butter and spoon into a crock. Choose from parsley, dill, thyme and chives, or create your own herb garden mixture.

Golden Parmesan Roasted Potatoes

*Pop the pan into the oven alongside a roast for
a homestyle dinner that can't be beat.*

1/4 c. all-purpose flour
1/4 c. grated Parmesan cheese
3/4 t. salt
1/8 t. pepper

6 potatoes, peeled and cut into
 wedges
1/3 c. butter, melted
Garnish: chopped fresh parsley

Place flour, cheese, salt and pepper in a large plastic zipping bag; mix
well. Add potato wedges; seal bag and shake to coat. Pour butter into a
13"x9" baking pan, tilting to coat; arrange potatoes in pan. Bake,
uncovered, at 375 degrees for one hour, or until potatoes are tender and
golden. Sprinkle with parsley just before serving. Serves 4 to 6.

Scalloped Zucchini

*You can always use another tasty way to serve zucchini! Choose medium
zucchini...they're more tender than the really large ones.*

4 to 5 zucchini, sliced and divided
1 onion, sliced and divided
10 to 12 slices pasteurized process
 cheese spread, divided

1 sleeve rectangular buttery
 crackers, crushed
1/2 c. butter, sliced

Layer half each of zucchini, onion and cheese slices in a buttered
13"x9" baking pan. Repeat layering; top with crackers and dot with butter.
Bake, uncovered, at 325 degrees until zucchini is tender, about 40 minutes.
Serves 8 to 10.

Golden Parmesan Roasted Potatoes

Kickin' Cajun Tilapia

Kickin' Cajun Tilapia

Resolving to eat more fish? Try this delicious dish! Tilapia is a mild, tasty fish, and this recipe really has a flavorful zip.

3 T. paprika
1 T. onion powder
1 t. cayenne pepper
1 t. dried thyme
1 t. dried oregano
1/2 t. celery salt

1/8 t. garlic powder
2 t. salt
2 t. pepper
4 tilapia fillets
2 T. oil
Garnish: lemon wedges

Mix seasonings in a shallow bowl or on a plate. Press both sides of tilapia fillets into seasoning mixture; let stand for 10 minutes. Heat oil in a skillet over medium heat. Cook fillets for 4 to 6 minutes, turning once, until fish flakes easily with a fork. Remove fish to a serving plate; garnish with lemon wedges. Serves 4.

A special touch when serving seafood. Wrap lemon halves in cheesecloth, tie with a colorful ribbon and set one on each plate. Guests can squeeze the lemon over their dishes...the cheesecloth prevents squirting and catches any seeds.

Garlicky Parmesan Asparagus

Savor the flavor of garden-fresh asparagus in this simple recipe...
nice with a baked ham or grilled fish.

1 T. butter
1/4 c. olive oil
2 cloves garlic, minced
1 lb. asparagus spears, trimmed

2 t. lemon juice
salt and pepper to taste
Garnish: shredded Parmesan
  cheese

Combine butter and oil in a skillet over medium heat. Add garlic; sauté for one to 2 minutes. Add asparagus and cook to desired tenderness, stirring occasionally, 7 to 10 minutes. Drain; sprinkle asparagus with lemon juice, salt and pepper. Arrange asparagus on a serving platter; sprinkle with cheese. Makes 4 servings.

Bake a panful of roasted vegetables alongside a casserole. Peel and slice zucchini, cauliflower, squash, asparagus or other veggies of your choice. Toss with olive oil and spread on a jelly-roll pan. Bake at 350 degrees for about 30 minutes, stirring occasionally, until tender.

Garlicky Parmesan Asparagus

Amanda's Chicken & Orzo

A great meal-in-one in about 20 minutes.

4 boneless, skinless chicken
  breasts
1 t. dried basil
salt and pepper to taste
4 T. olive oil, divided
2 zucchini, sliced

8-oz. pkg. orzo pasta, uncooked
1 T. butter, softened
2 T. red wine vinegar
Optional: 1 t. fresh dill, snipped
Garnish: lemon wedges

Season chicken with basil, salt and pepper; set aside. Heat 2 tablespoons oil in a skillet over medium heat. Add chicken to skillet and cook, turning once, for 12 minutes, or until juices run clear. Remove chicken to a plate; cover to keep warm. Add zucchini to skillet and cook for 3 minutes, or until crisp-tender. Meanwhile, cook orzo according to package directions; drain and stir in butter. Whisk together remaining oil, vinegar and dill, if using; drizzle over orzo and toss to mix. Season with additional salt and pepper, if desired. Serve chicken and zucchini with orzo, garnished with lemon wedges. Serves 4.

Sausage & Chicken Cassoulet

This savory casserole is full of wonderful flavors...better bring along some recipe cards to share!

1 lb. hot Italian ground pork
  sausage
1 c. carrot, peeled and thinly sliced
1 onion, diced
2 t. garlic, minced
1 c. red wine or beef broth
2 T. tomato paste

1 bay leaf
1 t. dried thyme
1 t. dried rosemary
salt and pepper to taste
2 c. cooked chicken, diced
2*15-oz. cans Great Northern
  beans

Brown sausage in a Dutch oven over medium heat; drain. Add carrot, onion and garlic. Sauté for 3 minutes. Add wine or broth, tomato paste and seasonings; bring to a boil. Remove from heat; stir in chicken and beans with liquid. Bake, covered, at 350 degrees for 45 minutes, or until bubbly. Discard bay leaf before serving. Serves 4 to 6.

Amanda's Chicken & Orzo

Ziti with Sausage & Zucchini

The whole family will love this simple supper...perfect with a slice of crusty bread!

16-oz. pkg. ziti pasta, uncooked
3/4 lb. Italian ground pork sausage
3 zucchini, thinly sliced
salt and pepper to taste

28-oz. can whole tomatoes
1/8 t. sugar
Garnish: grated Parmesan cheese

Cook pasta according to package directions; drain. Meanwhile, brown sausage in a skillet over medium heat. Drain and set aside sausage, reserving one tablespoon drippings in skillet. Add zucchini to skillet; season with salt and pepper. Sauté until zucchini is tender and golden, about 10 minutes. Stir in tomatoes with juice and sugar; bring to a boil, breaking up tomatoes with a spoon. Return sausage to skillet and reduce heat to low. Cover and cook until heated through, about 5 to 6 minutes. Serve over cooked pasta; sprinkle with Parmesan cheese. Serves 6.

Too much zucchini? Thinly slice or grate extra zucchini and freeze it in 2-cup portions. It'll be ready to add to your favorite recipes all winter long.

Ziti with Sausage & Zucchini

Pizza Potato Puff Casserole

Need something new for family pizza night? Everyone will love this quick & easy casserole!

1 lb. ground beef
1/4 c. onion, chopped
10-3/4 oz. can cream of
   mushroom soup
8-oz. can pizza sauce

12 to 15 slices pepperoni
1/2 c. green pepper, chopped
1 c. shredded mozzarella cheese
16-oz. pkg. frozen potato puffs

Brown beef and onion in a skillet over medium-high heat; drain. Stir in soup. Spoon beef mixture into a lightly greased 8"x8" baking pan. Spoon pizza sauce evenly over beef mixture; arrange pepperoni and green pepper over sauce. Sprinkle with cheese; arrange potato puffs over top. Cover with aluminum foil; bake at 375 degrees for 30 minutes. Uncover; bake an additional 15 to 20 minutes, until heated through. Serves 4.

Cheesy Vegetable Casserole

Vary this casserole with different blends of frozen vegetables...there's quite a few to choose from!

2 16-oz. pkgs. frozen stir-fry
   blend vegetables, thawed and
   drained
16-oz. pkg. pasteurized process
   cheese spread, cubed

1/4 c. milk
1 sleeve round buttery
   crackers, crushed
1/2 c. butter, melted

Place vegetables in a lightly greased 13"x9" baking pan; set aside. Melt cheese in a saucepan over low heat. Add milk and stir until smooth; pour over vegetables. Toss together cracker crumbs and melted butter; sprinkle over vegetables. Bake, uncovered, at 350 degrees for 20 to 25 minutes, until hot and golden on top. Makes 8 to 10 servings.

Pizza Potato Puff Casserole

When company is coming for dinner, tried & true is best! Use simple recipes you know will be a hit, rather than trying new recipes at the last minute. Guests will be happy, and you'll avoid tossing dishes that didn't turn out as expected.

Whip up a fresh salad for dinner tonight. Toss together mixed greens, cherry tomatoes and thinly sliced red onion in a salad bowl. Whisk together 1/4 cup each of balsamic vinegar and olive oil, then drizzle over salad...so zesty!

Try a new topping on casserole dishes...sprinkle on shredded cheese, buttered bread crumbs or crushed chow mein noodles. To keep the topping crisp, don't cover the casserole dish during baking.

Start a family tradition...have a candlelight dinner once a week with your children. A table set with lit tapers, snowy-white napkins and the best china will let your kids know they are special.

Desserts

Carrot Cake

Moist and delicious...just what carrot cake should be.

2 c. all-purpose flour
2 t. baking powder
1-1/2 t. baking soda
1 t. salt
2 t. cinnamon

3/4 c. oil
2 c. sugar
4 eggs, beaten
2 c. carrots, peeled and grated
15-1/4 oz. can crushed pineapple

Combine all ingredients; beat well and pour into a greased and floured Bundt® pan. Bake at 325 degrees for 40 to 45 minutes, until cake tests done with a toothpick. Cool; frost while still warm. Makes 12 to 15 servings.

Frosting:

1/2 c. butter, softened
8-oz. pkg. cream cheese, softened
1 t. vanilla extract

16-oz. pkg. powdered sugar
Optional: milk

Beat all ingredients together until smooth and creamy. If desired, stir in milk to a drizzling consistency.

Create a charming cake stand with thrift-store finds.
Attach a glass plate with epoxy glue to a short glass vase or candle stand for a base. Let dry completely before using. Clever!

Carrot Cake

Special Mocha Cupcakes

Desserts

Special Mocha Cupcakes

Invite your best girlfriend over for conversation, a mug of hot coffee and a cupcake...or two!

1-1/2 c. all-purpose flour
1 c. sugar
1/3 c. baking cocoa
1 t. baking soda
1/2 t. salt

2 eggs, beaten
1/2 c. brewed coffee, chilled
1/2 c. oil
1 T. vinegar
1 T. vanilla extract

Combine flour, sugar, cocoa, baking soda and salt in a large bowl; mix well and set aside. Combine remaining ingredients in a separate bowl; add to flour mixture and stir well. Fill paper-lined muffin cups 2/3 full. Bake at 350 degrees for 20 to 25 minutes. Cool in muffin tin on a wire rack for 10 minutes. Remove cupcakes to a wire rack; cool completely. Frost with Mocha Frosting. Makes one dozen.

Mocha Frosting:
3 T. semi-sweet chocolate chips
3 T. milk chocolate chips
1/3 c. butter, softened

2 c. powdered sugar
1 to 2 T. brewed coffee, chilled

Combine chocolate chips in a microwave-safe bowl. Microwave for 15 seconds and stir; repeat until melted. Stir until smooth. Transfer melted chocolate to a large bowl; stir in butter. Gradually beat in powdered sugar. Stir in coffee until smooth.

Peanut Butter Bars

Make a good thing even better...drizzle with melted chocolate. Scrumptious!

1-1/2 c. graham cracker crumbs
1 c. butter, melted
16-oz. pkg. powdered sugar

1 c. creamy peanut butter
12-oz. pkg. butterscotch chips

Combine graham cracker crumbs, butter, powdered sugar and peanut butter; mix well. Press into the bottom of a lightly greased 13"x9" baking pan; set aside. Melt butterscotch chips in a double boiler; spread over crumb mixture. Cover and refrigerate for several hours to overnight, until firm. Cut into bars. Makes 2 dozen.

Spiced Pumpkin Bars

*Dip a mini cookie cutter into cinnamon and lightly press
into the frosting...such a pretty touch!*

4 eggs, beaten	1 t. baking soda
1 c. oil	1/2 t. salt
2 c. sugar	2 t. cinnamon
15-oz. can pumpkin	1/2 t. ground ginger
2 c. all-purpose flour	1/2 t. nutmeg
2 t. baking powder	1/2 t. ground cloves

Mix together eggs, oil, sugar and pumpkin in a large bowl. Add remaining ingredients and mix well; pour into a greased and floured 18"x12" jelly-roll pan. Bake at 350 degrees for 30 to 40 minutes, until a toothpick comes out clean. Let cool; frost and cut into bars. Makes 1-1/2 to 2 dozen.

Cream Cheese Frosting:

8-oz. pkg. cream cheese, softened	1 t. vanilla extract
6 T. butter, softened	4 c. powdered sugar
1 T. milk	

Beat together cream cheese, butter, milk and vanilla; gradually stir in powdered sugar to a spreading consistency.

Take-out boxes are available in lots of festive colors and patterns.
Keep some handy for wrapping up food gifts in a jiffy...and for
sending home desserts with guests who just can't eat another bite!

Spiced Pumpkin Bars

Amish Pear Pie

Amish Pear Pie

Try this...you'll be surprised and delighted by the combination!

1/3 c. sugar
1 T. cornstarch
1/8 t. salt

5 c. pears, cored, peeled and sliced
9-inch pie crust
Optional: vanilla ice cream

Mix sugar, cornstarch and salt together; add pear slices and toss to coat. Spread in pie crust; sprinkle with Cheese Topping. Bake on lower oven rack at 425 degrees for 25 to 30 minutes, or until pears are tender. Serve with a scoop of ice cream, if desired. Makes 8 servings.

Cheese Topping:

1/2 c. all-purpose flour
1/4 t. salt
1/2 c. sugar

1/2 c. shredded sharp Cheddar
   cheese
1/4 c. butter, melted

Combine all ingredients; stir until mixture resembles coarse crumbs.

Host a neighborhood pie party! Invite everyone to tie on an apron and bring their best-loved pie to share, along with extra copies of the recipe. Bring home some new-to-you recipes... one of them just might become a favorite!

Cinnamon Poached Pears

A light dessert that's not too sweet, or serve as a delicious side dish for roast chicken.

4 pears
1 c. pear nectar
1 c. water
3/4 c. maple syrup

2 4-inch cinnamon sticks, slightly crushed
4 strips lemon zest

Peel and core pears from the bottom, leaving stems intact. Cut a thin slice off bottom so pears will stand up; set aside. Combine remaining ingredients in a saucepan. Bring to a boil over medium heat, stirring occasionally. Add pears, standing right-side up. Reduce heat and simmer, covered, for 20 to 30 minutes, until tender. Remove pears from pan. Continue to simmer sauce in pan until reduced to 3/4 cup, about 15 minutes. Serve pears drizzled with sauce. Serves 4.

Place unripened pears in a plastic zipping bag with a ripe banana... the pears will ripen in no time.

Cinnamon Poached Pears

Apple-Cranberry Crisp

Desserts

Apple-Cranberry Crisp

A must-have at our holiday dinners.

6 c. Golden Delicious or Winesap
   apples, peeled, cored and sliced
3 c. fresh cranberries
1 c. sugar
2 t. cinnamon

1 to 2 t. lemon juice
3/4 c. butter, sliced and divided
1 c. all-purpose flour
1 c. brown sugar, packed
Garnish: vanilla ice cream

Toss together apple slices, cranberries, sugar and cinnamon. Spread in a greased 13"x9" baking pan. Sprinkle with lemon juice; dot with 1/4 cup butter. Blend remaining butter with flour and brown sugar until crumbly; sprinkle over apple mixture. Bake at 350 degrees for one hour. Serve warm with ice cream. Serves 10 to 12.

Too-Easy Cherry Cobbler

Put this yummy cobbler in the oven just before you sit down to dinner...
it'll be ready when you are!

2 21-oz. cans cherry pie filling
15-oz. can dark sweet cherries,
   drained
4 T. all-purpose flour, divided
1/2 t. almond extract
5 slices white bread, crusts
   trimmed

1-1/4 c. sugar
1/2 c. butter, melted
1 egg, beaten
1-1/2 t. lemon zest

In a large bowl, stir together pie filling, cherries, 2 tablespoons flour and extract. Transfer to a lightly greased 8"x8" baking pan. Cut each slice of bread into 5 strips; arrange strips over fruit mixture. In a separate bowl, stir together sugar, butter, egg, remaining flour and lemon zest. Drizzle over bread strips. Bake at 350 degrees for 35 to 45 minutes, or until golden and bubbly. Serves 6.

Scrumptious Cranberry Blondies

*We look forward to fall when cranberries are in season,
just so we can make these yummy blondies!*

1/2 c. butter, softened	2 eggs, beaten
1/2 c. sugar	1 t. vanilla extract
1/2 c. brown sugar, packed	1 c. all-purpose flour
3/4 t. baking powder	1/2 c. sweetened dried cranberries
1/4 t. baking soda	1/2 c. white chocolate chips
1/4 t. salt	1 c. fresh cranberries

In a large bowl, beat together butter, sugars, baking powder, baking soda
and salt. Beat in eggs and vanilla. Mix in flour, dried cranberries and
chocolate chips. Line a 9"x9" baking pan with aluminum foil, leaving a few
inches on sides for handles; spray with non-stick vegetable spray. Spread
dough in pan; lightly press fresh cranberries into dough. Bake at 350 degrees
for 25 to 30 minutes, until a toothpick tests clean. Cool; lift foil to remove
from pan. Cut into bars. Makes one dozen.

For a simple (and tasty!) garnish for cookie bars, melt 1/2 cup white
chocolate chips with 1-1/2 teaspoons shortening. Drizzle over bars
before cutting and watch the treats disappear.

Scrumptious Cranberry Blondies

Streusel-Topped Raspberry Bars

Streusel-Topped Raspberry Bars

Just the thing for a mid-morning coffee break with friends!

2-1/4 c. all-purpose flour
1 c. sugar
1 c. chopped pecans
1 c. butter, softened

1 egg
1 c. raspberry preserves
Garnish: powdered sugar

Combine flour, sugar, pecans, butter and egg in a large bowl. Beat with an electric mixer on low speed for 2 to 3 minutes. Set aside 2 cups of mixture for topping. Press remaining mixture into bottom of a greased 13"x9" baking pan. Spread preserves over top; sprinkle with reserved mixture. Bake at 350 degrees for 40 to 50 minutes, until lightly golden. Cool completely; cut into bars and sprinkle with powdered sugar. Makes 2 dozen.

Bake up some bar cookies or brownies, then cut, wrap and freeze them individually. Later you can pull out what you need for last-minute lunches...or when you just need a goodie!

Dark Chocolate Pecan Pie

*Decadent, rich and fantastic! You'll save room
for dessert whenever this is on the menu.*

1-1/2 c. pecan halves
1-1/2 c. dark chocolate chips
1 T. all-purpose flour
1/2 c. butter, softened
1/2 c. light brown sugar, packed
3 eggs

1/2 c. dark corn syrup
2 t. vanilla extract
1/4 t. salt
9-inch pie crust, baked
Garnish: whipped topping

In a bowl, stir together pecans, chocolate chips and flour; set aside. In another bowl, beat butter and brown sugar until well blended. Beat in eggs, one at a time. Mix in corn syrup, vanilla and salt, just until blended. Stir in pecan mixture. Pour into baked pie crust. Bake at 325 degrees for 55 to 60 minutes, until a toothpick inserted in center comes out with just melted chocolate. Cool on a wire rack; center will set as it cools. Chill until serving time. Garnish with whipped topping. Makes 8 servings.

234

After a hearty meal, offer mini portions of rich cake, cobbler or pie layered in small glasses with whipped topping and a crunchy topping. Guests can take "just a taste" of something sweet or sample several yummy treats.

Dark Chocolate Pecan Pie

Harvest Celebration Cake

Harvest Celebration Cake

Such a pretty cake and so delicious! For another beautiful presentation, pour batter into a greased and floured Bundt® pan; bake at 350 degrees for about one hour.

1-1/2 c. sugar
1/2 c. brown sugar, packed
2 t. baking soda
1/2 t. salt
2 t. cinnamon
1/4 t. nutmeg
1/4 t. ground ginger

1 c. oil
1/2 t. vanilla extract
4 eggs, beaten
2 c. all-purpose flour
15-oz. can pumpkin
1 apple, peeled, cored and chopped
Optional: 1/2 c. chopped walnuts

In a large bowl, combine sugars, baking soda, salt and spices; mix well. Stir in oil, vanilla and eggs. Add flour, 1/2 cup at a time, beating after each addition. Mix in pumpkin; fold in apple and nuts, if using. Divide batter among 3 greased and floured 9" round cake pans. Bake at 350 degrees for 30 to 35 minutes, until cake tests clean with a toothpick. Let cool; assemble cake with Frosting. Serves 10 to 12.

237

Frosting:

1/2 c. butter, softened
8-oz. pkg. cream cheese, softened

1 t. vanilla extract
16-oz. pkg. powdered sugar

Beat all ingredients together until smooth and creamy.

Forget about anything fussy...
enjoy dessert outside and let the
crumbs fall where they may!

Coffee Cream Brownies

Go ahead and serve these with a scoop of ice cream...so good!

3 1-oz. sqs. unsweetened baking
  chocolate, chopped
1/2 c. plus 2 T. butter, softened
  and divided
2 eggs, beaten
1 c. sugar
1 t. vanilla extract

2/3 c. all-purpose flour
1/4 t. baking soda
1 t. instant coffee granules
1/3 c. plus 1 T. whipping cream,
  divided
1 c. powdered sugar
1 c. semi-sweet chocolate chips

In a saucepan over low heat, melt baking chocolate and 1/2 cup butter;
let cool. In a bowl, beat eggs, sugar and vanilla. Stir in chocolate mixture.
Combine flour and baking soda; add to chocolate mixture. Spread in a
greased 8"x8" baking pan. Bake at 350 degrees for 25 to 30 minutes;
let cool. In a bowl, stir coffee granules into one tablespoon cream until
dissolved. Beat in remaining butter and powdered sugar until creamy;
spread over brownies. In a saucepan over low heat, stir and melt chocolate
chips and remaining cream until thickened. Spread over cream layer. Let set
and cut into squares. Makes one dozen.

Coffee Cream Brownies

Giant Chocolate Malt Cookies

Giant Chocolate Malt Cookies

The next best thing to a good old-fashioned malted shake!

1 c. butter-flavored shortening
1-1/4 c. brown sugar, packed
1/2 c. malted milk powder
2 T. chocolate syrup
1 T. vanilla extract
1 egg, beaten

2 c. all-purpose flour
1 t. baking soda
1/2 t. salt
1-1/2 c. semi-sweet chocolate
   chunks
1 c. milk chocolate chips

In a large bowl, blend shortening, brown sugar, malted milk powder, syrup and vanilla for 2 minutes. Add egg; blend well and set aside. In a separate bowl, mix together flour, baking soda and salt; gradually blend into shortening mixture. Fold in chocolates; shape dough into 2-inch balls. Arrange 3 inches apart on ungreased baking sheets; bake at 375 degrees for 12 to 14 minutes. Cool on baking sheets for 2 minutes before removing to a wire rack to cool completely. Makes 1-1/2 dozen.

241

Make sure to have lots of extra chocolate chips, nuts and other cookie-baking goodies for sneaking, especially if you have little helpers lending a hand!

Double Peanut Cookies

For all the peanut lovers out there! Smooth peanut cookies with crunchy roasted peanuts...so good.

1 c. all-purpose flour
1/2 t. baking soda
1/2 c. shortening
1/2 c. creamy peanut butter
1/2 c. sugar

1/2 c. brown sugar, packed
1 egg, beaten
1/2 c. salted dry-roasted peanuts,
    coarsely chopped

In a bowl, mix together flour and baking soda; set aside. In a separate large bowl, beat shortening and peanut butter until well blended. Add sugars; beat until fluffy. Beat in egg. Stir in flour mixture until well blended; stir in peanuts. Drop by rounded teaspoonfuls, 2 inches apart, onto ungreased baking sheets; flatten slightly. Bake at 350 degrees for 10 to 12 minutes, until lightly golden. Cool on baking sheets for about 5 minutes; remove to wire racks to cool completely. Makes 3 dozen.

English Toffee Cookie Bars

A lovely take-along dessert...you're sure to be asked for the recipe!

1 c. butter, softened
1 c. brown sugar, packed
1 egg yolk
1 t. vanilla extract

2 c. all-purpose flour
8 1-1/2 oz. milk chocolate candy
    bars, broken into pieces
1 c. chopped walnuts

In a bowl, blend butter and brown sugar. Add egg yolk and vanilla; mix well. Add flour; mix well. Pat dough into a sheet in an ungreased 15"x10" jelly-roll pan. Bake at 350 degrees for about 18 to 20 minutes, until edges are lightly golden. Remove from oven; immediately top with chocolate pieces. Let stand for a few minutes, until chocolate melts; spread with a spatula. Sprinkle with chopped nuts; cut into squares. Makes 2-1/2 to 3 dozen.

Double Peanut Cookies

Fancy Caramel Apples

Desserts

Fancy Caramel Apples

For a new twist, try dipping the bottom half of caramel-coated apples in melted chocolate and then rolling in chopped nuts.

6 wooden treat sticks
6 tart apples
14-oz. pkg. caramels, unwrapped
2 T. milk

Garnish: colored candy sprinkles, mini chocolate chips, sunflower seeds

Insert sticks into tops of apples. Place apples in the freezer to chill while caramel coating is being made. Combine caramels and milk in a microwave-safe bowl; microwave on high for 3 minutes, stirring once. Allow to cool briefly. Remove apples from freezer. Dip into caramel coating, then into desired garnish. Place apples on a lightly buttered baking sheet to cool. Chill in freezer to set up if necessary. Makes 6 servings.

No-Fuss Caramel Corn

So much tastier than store-bought caramel corn! Wrap it up in small bags for parties.

12 c. popped popcorn
Optional: 1-1/2 c. peanuts
1 c. brown sugar, packed
1/2 c. butter, sliced

1/4 c. light corn syrup
1/2 t. salt
1/2 t. baking soda

Place popcorn in a large brown paper bag; add peanuts, if using, and set aside. Combine brown sugar, butter, corn syrup and salt in a microwave-safe glass bowl. Microwave on high setting for 3 to 4 minutes, stirring after each minute, until mixture comes to a boil. Microwave for 2 additional minutes without stirring; stir in baking soda. Pour mixture over popcorn; close bag and shake well. Seal bag; microwave for 1-1/2 minutes. Shake bag well and pour popcorn into a roaster pan; cool and stir. Store in an airtight container. Makes about 12 cups.

Peaches & Cream Dessert

Peaches & Cream Dessert

Peaches never tasted so good!

3/4 c. all-purpose flour
3.4-oz. pkg. instant vanilla
   pudding mix
1 t. baking powder
1 egg, beaten
1/2 c. milk
3 T. butter, melted and
   slightly cooled

16-oz. can sliced peaches, drained
   and 1/3 c. juice reserved
8-oz. pkg. cream cheese, softened
1/2 c. plus 1 T. sugar, divided
1/2 t. cinnamon

In a bowl, combine flour, dry pudding mix and baking powder; set aside. In a separate bowl, whisk egg, milk and butter together; add to flour mixture. Mix well; spread in a greased 8"x8" baking pan. Chop peaches and sprinkle over batter; set aside. Blend together cream cheese, 1/2 cup sugar and reserved peach juice until smooth; spoon over peaches. Mix together remaining sugar and cinnamon; sprinkle on top. Bake at 350 degrees for 45 minutes. Makes 9 servings.

247

Happiness being a dessert so sweet,
May life give you more than you can ever eat.
-Irish Toast

Marble Cheesecake

Desserts

Marble Cheesecake

Sure to be a hit at your next party or get-together!

1 c. graham cracker crumbs
3 T. sugar
3 T. butter, melted
3 8-oz. pkgs. cream cheese,
  softened
3/4 c. sugar

3 T. all-purpose flour
1 t. vanilla extract
3 eggs, beaten
1-oz. sq. unsweetened baking
  chocolate, melted and
  cooled slightly

In a bowl, combine cracker crumbs, sugar and melted butter; press into the bottom of an ungreased 9" springform pan. Bake at 350 degrees for 10 minutes. With an electric mixer on medium speed, beat cream cheese, sugar, flour and vanilla until well blended. Beat in eggs. Remove one cup of batter to a separate bowl and blend in melted chocolate. Spoon plain and chocolate batters alternately over crust. Use a knife to swirl through batter several times for marble effect. Bake at 450 degrees for 10 minutes. Reduce oven to 250 degrees; bake an additional 30 minutes. Loosen pan's rim, but do not remove. Let cool; remove rim. Chill until serving time. Serves 8 to 10.

For best results when baking, let eggs stand at room temperature at least 30 minutes before using. Short on time? Place eggs in a bowl of warm water up to 15 minutes.

Molasses Crinkles

Molasses Crinkles

An old-fashioned cookie jar favorite.

3/4 c. shortening
1 c. brown sugar, packed
1 egg, beaten
1/4 c. molasses
2-1/4 c. all-purpose flour

1/4 t. baking soda
1 t. cinnamon
1 t. ground ginger
Garnish: sugar

In a large bowl, mix shortening, brown sugar, egg and molasses. Stir in remaining ingredients except garnish in the order listed. Form dough into one-inch balls. Dip tops in sugar and place on ungreased baking sheets. Gently press a thumbprint into the center of each ball. Sprinkle one to 4 drops of water in each indentation. Bake at 350 degrees for 10 to 12 minutes. Let cool on a wire rack. Makes 4 dozen.

Pineapple Goodie Bars

*If the kids just told you about tomorrow's bake sale or potluck,
this will get you out of a jam...fast!*

18-oz. tube refrigerated sugar
  cookie dough
1 c. chopped pecans
1/2 c. candied pineapple, chopped

1/2 c. sweetened dried cranberries
1/2 c. butterscotch chips
1/2 c. sweetened flaked coconut

Place cookie dough in a bowl; stir until softened. Add remaining ingredients except coconut; mix well. Pat mixture evenly into a greased 13"x9" baking pan. Sprinkle coconut over top and press lightly. Bake at 325 degrees for 20 minutes, or until golden. Cool; cut into bars. Makes 2 dozen.

Scoops of ice cream are perfect alongside warm cobblers and pies. To make them ahead of time, simply scoop servings and arrange on a baking sheet, then pop into the freezer. When frozen, store scoops in a freezer bag, then remove as many as needed at dessert time.

For a festive dessert that's quick as a wink, layer fresh berries with creamy vanilla pudding in stemmed glasses.

Turn your favorite cake recipe into cupcakes...terrific for bake sales. Fill greased muffin cups 2/3 full. Bake at the same temperature as in the recipe, but cut the baking time by 1/3 to 1/2. From a cake recipe that makes two layers, you'll get 24 to 30 cupcakes.

Don't hide a pretty glass cake stand in the cupboard! Use it to show off several of Mom's best dessert plates or arrange colorful, seasonal fruit on top.

Index

Appetizers

Beverages

Breads

Breakfasts

Desserts

Index

Index

Soups & Stews

all-American ☀ just like Mom's ⊕ hearty

old-fashioned

laughter

paʞooɔǝɯoɥ Good food ǝnɹʇ ⅋ pǝᴉɹʇ

satisfying

homestyle

U.S. to Metric Recipe Equivalents

Volume Measurements

1/4 teaspoon	1 mL
1/2 teaspoon	2 mL
1 teaspoon	5 mL
1 tablespoon = 3 teaspoons	15 mL
2 tablespoons = 1 fluid ounce	30 mL
1/4 cup	60 mL
1/3 cup	75 mL
1/2 cup = 4 fluid ounces	125 mL
1 cup = 8 fluid ounces	250 mL
2 cups = 1 pint =16 fluid ounces	500 mL
4 cups = 1 quart	1 L

Weights

1 ounce	30 g
4 ounces	120 g
8 ounces	225 g
16 ounces = 1 pound	450 g

Oven Temperatures

300° F	150° C
325° F	160° C
350° F	180° C
375° F	190° C
400° F	200° C
450° F	230° C

Baking Pan Sizes

Square	
8x8x2 inches	2 L = 20x20x5 cm
9x9x2 inches	2.5 L = 23x23x5 cm
Rectangular	
13x9x2 inches	3.5 L = 33x23x5 cm

Loaf	
9x5x3 inches	2 L = 23x13x7 cm
Round	
8x1-1/2 inches	1.2 L = 20x4 cm
9x1-1/2 inches	1.5 L = 23x4 cm